AMAZING STRUCTURES

Written by
Michael Pollard

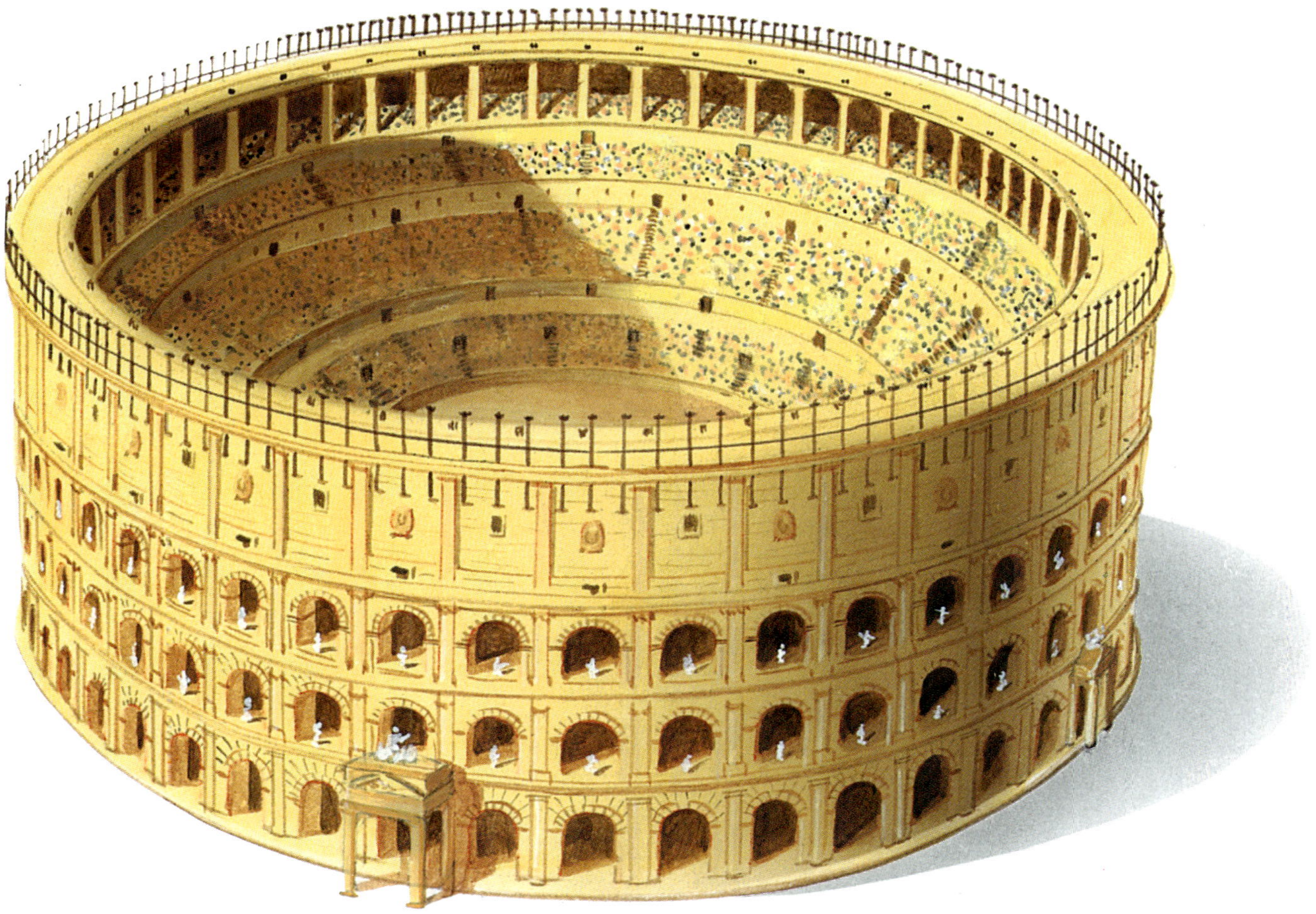

Vineyard BOOKS

ACKNOWLEDGEMENTS

Illustrated by
Julian Baker, Bob Corley (Artist Partners), Robert Farnworth, Dave Higginson (Northern Art Collection), Steve Noon (Garden Studios), Julia Osorno, John Rogers (Ian Fleming & Associates), Roger Stewart (Kevin Jones Associates), Andrew Wheatcroft (Virgil Pomfret Agency), Sean Wilkinson

The Publishers would also like to thank the following for their assistance
Blackpool Pleasure Beach Ltd
Eiffel Tower archivist
Empire State Building
Jodrell Bank, for information on the VLA Radio Telescope
Statoil, for information on Gullfaks C
Thames Barrier Publicity
United States Information Service at the American Embassy, London
Vale Royal Borough Council, for information on the Anderton Boat Lift
Wirth Howden Tunnelling for information on the Channel Tunnel

Published in 1996 by
Vineyard Books, an imprint of
Andromeda Oxford Limited
11–15 The Vineyard
Abingdon
Oxon OX14 3PX

Planned and produced by
Andromeda Oxford Limited
11–15 The Vineyard
Abingdon
Oxon OX14 3PX

Reprinted 1997

ISBN 1-871869-84-6

Printed in Italy

Contents

What is a structure?

A structure is an object that has been designed and built for a special purpose. Thousands of years ago, people built the world's first structures, their homes, out of the branches and leaves of trees. As they learned to make and use tools, they began to build larger structures using a wider variety of materials. Places of worship were among the first large structures to be built. The Ancient Egyptians built temples in which to worship their gods. They also worshipped their rulers and built huge palaces for them to live in. When Egyptian rulers died, they were buried in pyramids with their treasures alongside them.

Many modern structures such as skyscrapers, oil-rigs and space stations have been built as working environments. Others, like tunnels and bridges, carry roads or railways. Another group of structures, the Eiffel Tower and Statue of Liberty among them, were built as monuments to celebrate important events. Over the centuries of human history large structures, from the Great Wall of China to today's structures in space, mark the achievements of gifted designers, builders and craftspeople.

PLACES OF WORSHIP

Temples and churches are mostly grand structures with domes, towers or spires that soar upwards towards the sky. During the twelfth and thirteenth centuries, there was a great surge of cathedral building in the Christian countries of western Europe. With their lofty vaulted roofs, buttressed walls and high arches, the new cathedrals achieved a splendour that had not been seen in Europe before.

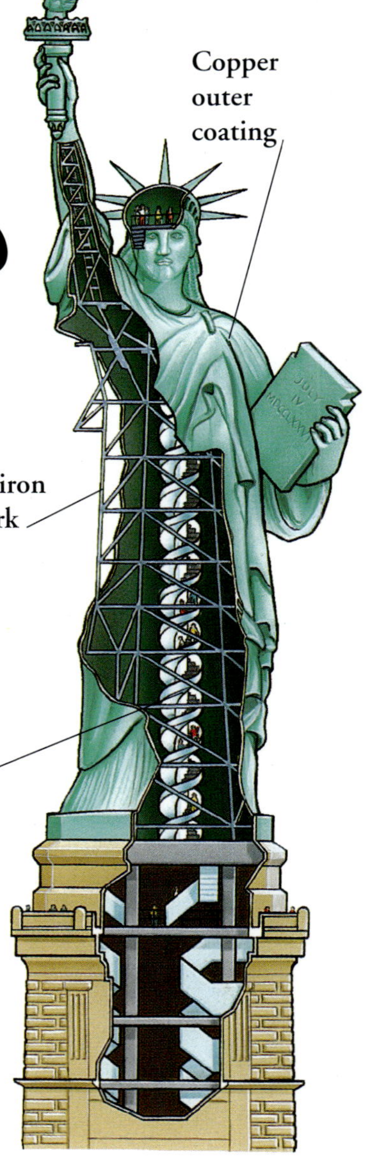

MONUMENTS

For thousands of years monuments have been built to commemorate events, such as victory in battle, or the achievements of well-known people. Memorials and statues are a familiar sight in many towns and cities, and some statues are famous worldwide. The Statue of Liberty, which stands in New York Harbour, was erected to celebrate the hundredth anniversary of the United States' independence from Britain.

BUILDING A STRUCTURE

No matter how much machinery is available, a skilled workforce has always been essential for building a structure. The pyramids of Ancient Egypt were built over 4,000 years ago, by a huge force of workers who laboured for years to build them, using only the simplest hand-tools. Over 70 pyramids have survived – a tribute to the Ancient Egyptians' building skills.

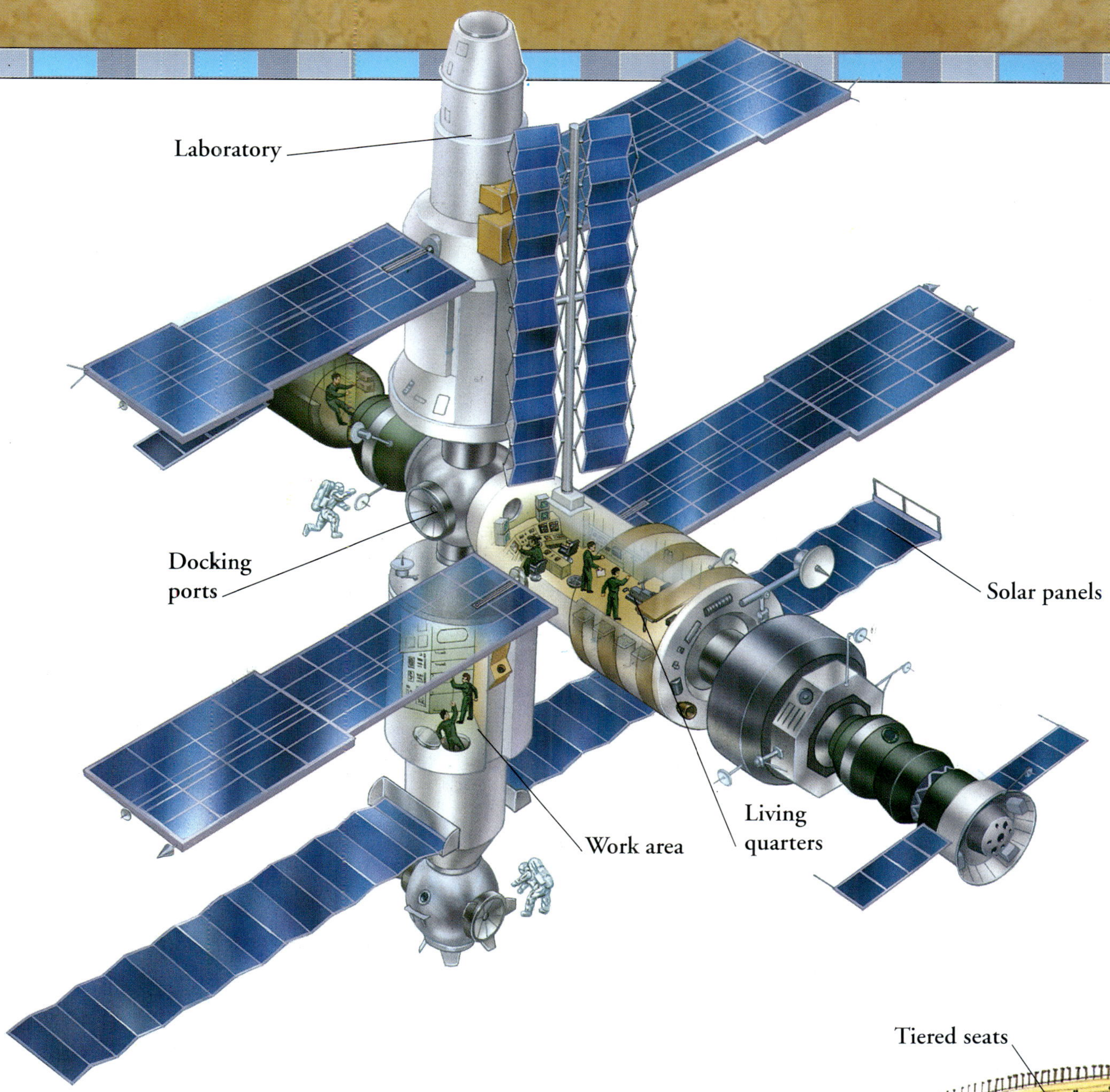

PLACES TO LIVE AND WORK

Our planet is so crowded that in some cities, such as New York and Hong Kong, the solution has been to build upwards. Nowadays millions of people live and work in skyscrapers. These glittering towers of concrete, glass and steel are some of the world's most exciting buildings. Out in space there are some amazing structures, too, such as the *Mir* Space Station, which is designed for long-term living in space. Cosmonauts have stayed there for up to a year before returning to Earth.

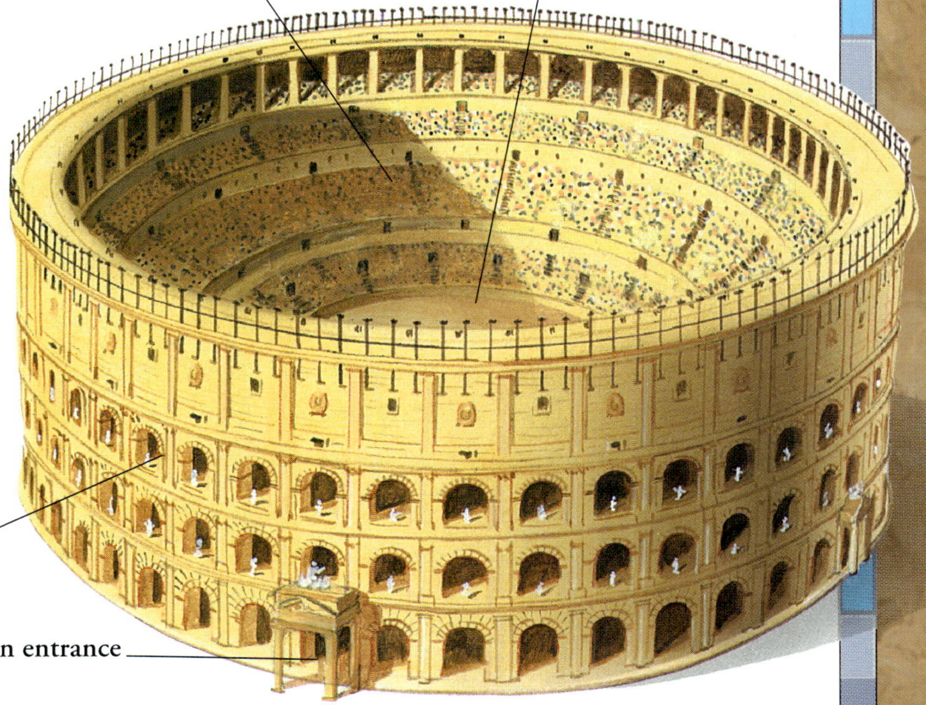

TRANSPORT SYSTEMS

Since the start of the Industrial Revolution in the eighteenth century, more and more structures have been needed to carry goods and people from place to place. Some transport systems are built when they are needed, while others must wait until the technological challenges have been overcome. A tunnel link between Britain and mainland Europe was a dream of engineers for almost 200 years. The Channel Tunnel, which was completed in 1993, remains one of the great engineering achievements of the twentieth century.

PLACES OF ENTERTAINMENT

As well as buildings for living and working, there are plenty of places for having fun. All over the world there are theatres, opera houses, cinemas, concert halls, sports stadiums, amusement parks and art galleries, each with its individual design requirements. Many places of entertainment need to accommodate seating for large numbers of people. The Colosseum, one of the finest buildings of Ancient Rome still standing, was an oval amphitheatre. It could seat up to 50,000 people who came to see a variety of entertainments, including gladiator contests.

Development of structures

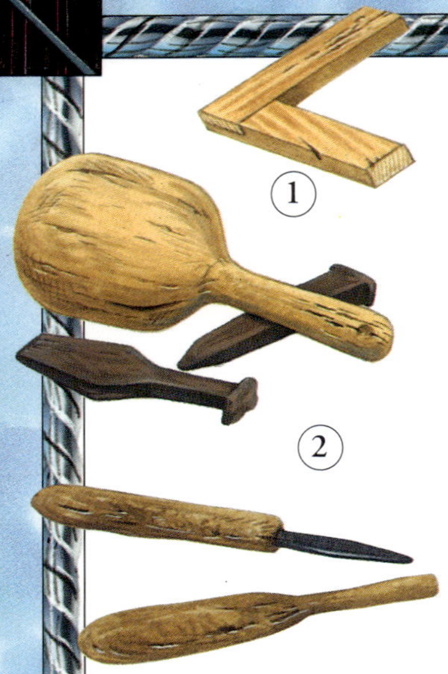

The history of large structures shows how the development of new materials and the invention of tools enabled designers and builders to take on new challenges. Until about 200 years ago, stone, brick and wood were the main building materials. From about 1800, iron and then steel were increasingly used in large structures. The twentieth century brought the use of reinforced and pre-stressed concrete, as well as a variety of plastics. All these materials made new kinds of structures possible.

STONEMASONS' TOOLS

This selection of ancient stonemasons' tools includes: a square (1) and a variety of mallets, wedges and chisels (2). A favourite material for making tools before the Iron Age was a hard stone called dolerite. Stone tools did not keep their edge for long, so stonemasons had teams of helpers to re-sharpen their tools and make new ones.

SCULPTING

Large stone structures such as those of the ancient world lent themselves to decoration with patterns, figures and inscriptions carved painstakingly out of the stonework. The sculptor's craft was highly valued.

DESIGN CHANGES

Designers have always looked for ways of improving structures. The first lengths of the Great Wall of China were made of earth, but when the Emperor wanted a stronger wall the design was improved to include stone foundations, with stone and brick walls and a brick pavement along the top.

MAKING BRICKS

Bricks were first used in places where stone was hard to find or difficult to transport. The first bricks were tablets of clay and straw that were allowed to harden in the sun. Soon it was found that bricks were stronger if the clay was baked in a fire or an oven. A mortar made from mud was used to hold the bricks in place.

GOING UP

Throughout recorded history, mankind has constantly developed new building materials, and invented new building techniques, to create ever more impressive structures.

c.2565 BC: Completion of the Great Pyramid at Giza.

AD 72–80: The Colosseum in Rome was an early example of the use of arches to carry great weights, enabling tall structures to be built.

1170: Krak des Chevaliers, Syria, a huge Crusader Castle, featured hidden passages and 8.5-metre-thick walls.

1779: First use of iron in structural building in a bridge at Ironbridge, England.

1818: Marc Isambard Brunel invented the tunnelling shield, which was first used to tunnel under the River Thames in London.

WELDING AND RIVETING

The Industrial Revolution in the nineteenth century opened up new opportunities in construction. The use of iron and steel meant that ways had to be found of joining pieces of metal together. Two of the methods used are welding (1) and riveting (2).

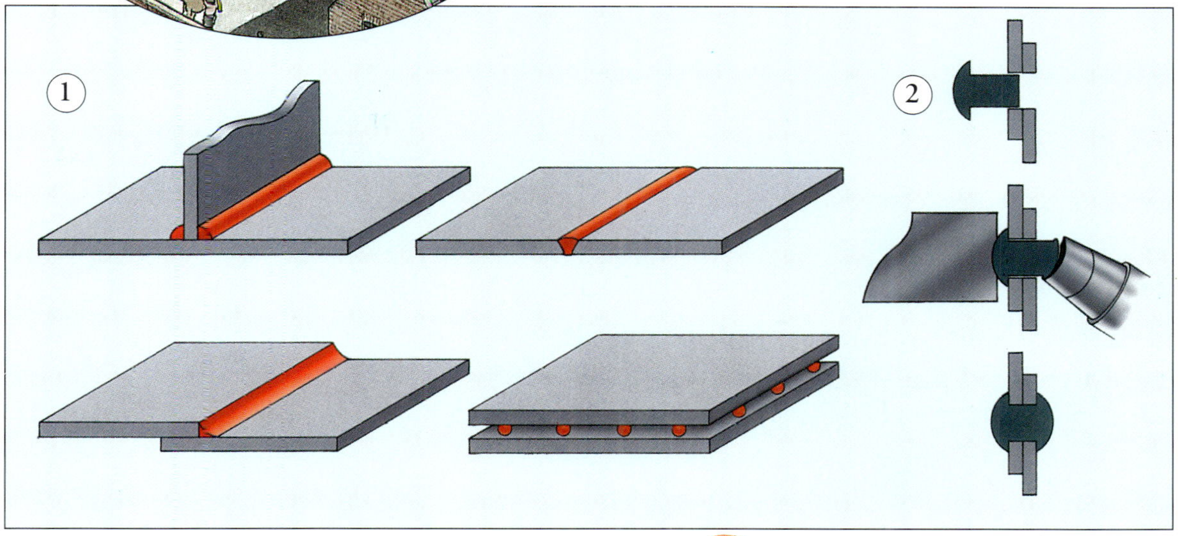

CRANES AND CANTILEVERS

Tower cranes lift materials, or even complete modules for a high-rise building, into place. They work on the same principle as a cantilever bridge, where the weight on one end of a beam supports the other end.

NEW CHALLENGES

From the 1960s onwards, the discovery of oil from reserves under the sea presented structural engineers with new challenges. They had to design oil rigs that would resist salt-water corrosion and stand up to stormy weather in open water. Oil rigs are massively built, with a steel framework attached to a heavy concrete base secured to the sea bed.

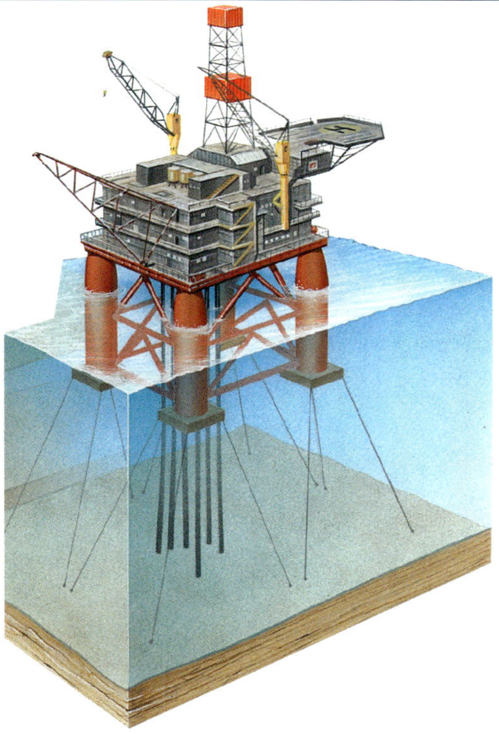

TUNNELLING

The history of modern tunnels began in 1818 when the tunnelling shield was invented, making it possible to tunnel through soft ground. In 1861 compressed-air drilling machines were introduced, followed in 1867 by dynamite, a more efficient explosive.

1868: Reinforced concrete invented when Joseph Monier, a French gardener, strengthened concrete by incorporating iron rods.

1885: World's first steel-framed building, the Home Insurance Building in Chicago, USA, built. Although only ten storeys high, it is recognised as the world's first skyscraper.

1889: Architecture and engineering combined to create the Eiffel Tower, France, a riveted iron structure.

1970s: The discovery of undersea oil and gas reserves resulted in the building of giant ocean platforms hundreds of metres tall that can withstand the fiercest storms.

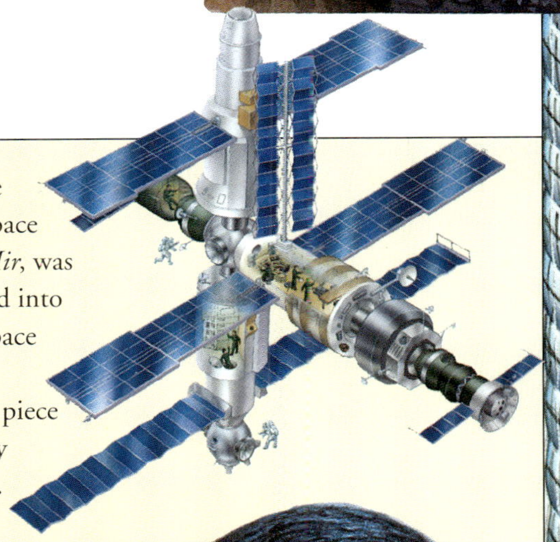

1986: The Russian Space Station, *Mir*, was transported into orbit by space craft and assembled piece by piece by astronauts.

1993: Completion of the Channel Tunnel, the largest-ever construction project in Europe.

Great Pyramid

"It shuts out the sky and the horizon. It shuts out all the other pyramids. It shuts out everything but the sense of awe and wonder."
Amelia B. Edwards
A Thousand Miles Up the Nile 1877

MAGIC EYE

The Egyptian sun-god, Horus, was worshipped and feared by the Ancient Egyptians, and his symbol, the magic eye, was used to ward off evil. The first pyramid, built as a burial place for King Djoser in about 2630 BC, was thought to represent a huge stairway for the king to climb to join the sun-god Horus in the sky.

In Ancient Egypt between 2630 BC and 1640 BC, when a pharaoh or his queen died, their mummified bodies were placed in stone tombs, called pyramids. The Egyptians believed that the spirits of the dead would travel from these tombs to the next world. At 148 metres high the Great Pyramid at Giza, near modern-day Cairo, is the tallest of the Egyptian pyramids, and the oldest of the Seven Wonders of the Ancient World. The Great Pyramid is the tomb of King Khufu, sometimes called by his Greek name, Cheops. No-one knows the exact dates of Khufu's birth and death, but the Great Pyramid, which was built in readiness for his death, was finished in about 2565 BC.

Khufu's Pyramid was built from more than two million blocks of stone and may have taken 20 years to build. The stone was brought by boat from the quarries, and then dragged to the site on sledges. Thousands of people worked on the building. The labourers were not slaves, but free Egyptians who worked on the pyramids as an act of worship to their king. They worked during the time of year when the land near the River Nile was flooded and no farming could be done.

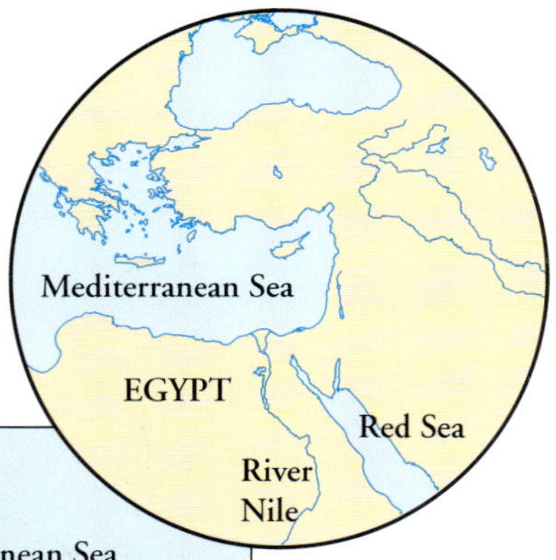

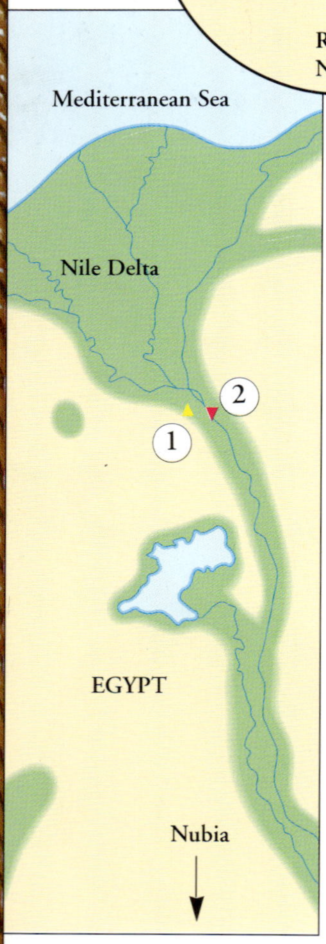

NILE VALLEY

The civilisation of Ancient Egypt grew up along 1,000 kilometres of the fertile River Nile between Nubia and the Nile Delta, where the river flows into the Mediterranean Sea. For almost 4,000 years, the Great Pyramid (1) was the tallest structure in the world. Beside it is the carved stone figure of the Sphinx (2).

ROBBERS

The pharaohs of Ancient Egypt were buried with their personal belongings. These included jewellery, gold ornaments and richly decorated furniture. About 500 years after Khufu's death, robbers broke into the pyramids and stripped them of their valuables. They even tore open some of the mummies to expose the kings' bodies, which then decayed.

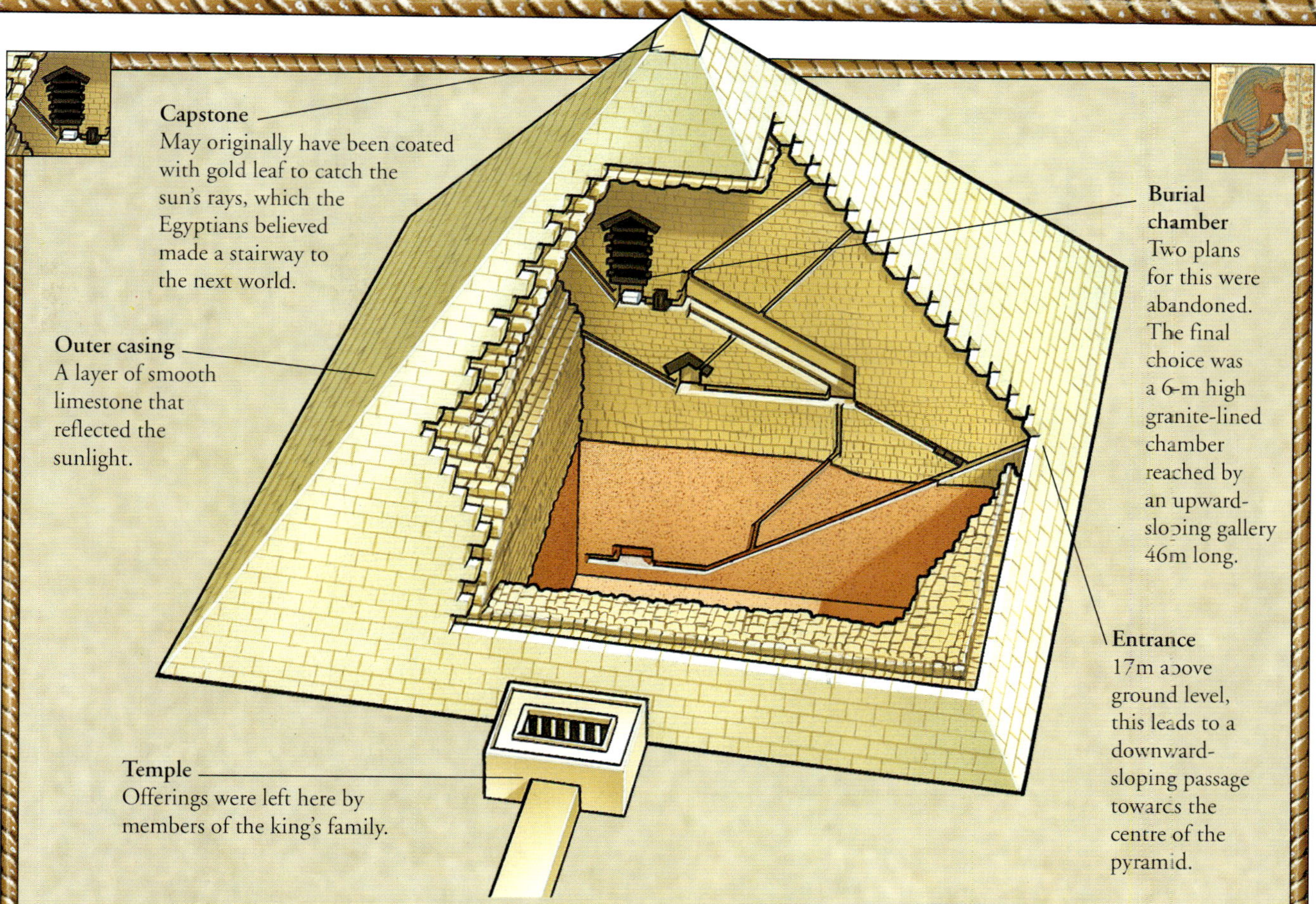

Khufu's Pyramid contains 2.3 million blocks of stone. The largest block weighs 15 tonnes, but most are about 2.5 tonnes in weight. Each side is 233m long at the base of the Pyramid. The base covers more than five hectares of ground.

THE SPHINX

The Great Pyramid is one of three large pyramids at Giza. Completing the group of monuments is the great stone human-headed lion, known as the Sphinx. Experts once thought that the Sphinx's head had been given the features of Khufu's son Khafre, who was buried in the second large pyramid. But they now think that the Sphinx may actually be much older than the Great Pyramid. The figure, which is over 57 metres long, was possibly intended to guard the entrance to the Nile valley.

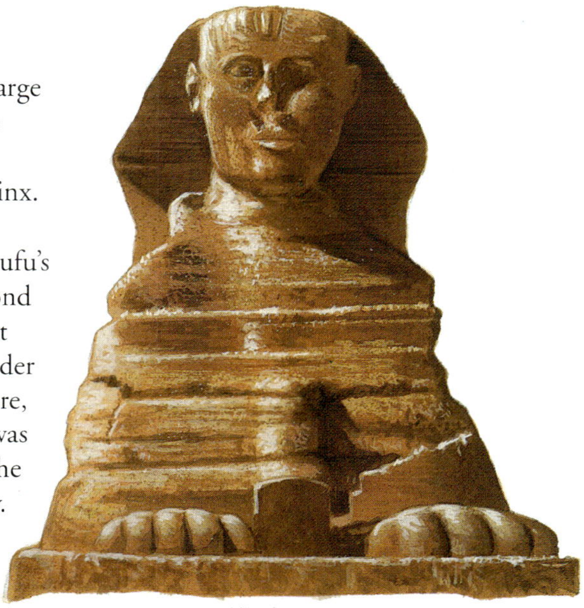

BURYING THE PHARAOH

The burial of a pharaoh began with the arrival of his body by boat at a temple on the Nile. From there, priests led the mourners to the pyramid entrance and then through passages to the burial chamber. When the pharaoh's mummified body had been arranged with his treasures, the burial chamber was sealed with blocks of stone.

Great Wall of China

"It is a supremely wonderful sight! To think that these walls, built in apparently inaccessible places, are the work of man makes it seem like a dream."
Ludovic Herbert *A Voyage Round the World* 1872

Throughout history, until recently, China's northern borders have been the target of attacks by invaders from the mountains to the north. The Great Wall of China is evidence of the Chinese Empire's long struggle to defend its northern provinces. It is by far the longest wall in the world, with its main length and side branches totalling more than 6,000 kilometres.

The Great Wall was begun about 300 BC, when the first separate parts, made of earth, were built by warring states across areas vulnerable to raiders. Then, in 221 BC, the first emperor of a united China ordered these short lengths to be transformed into a continuous stone wall. A force of 300,000 slaves took 20 years to complete the task. Soldiers were posted in the watchtowers that were placed every 100 to 200 metres. From there, a close watch was kept for raiders from the north, and a chain of beacons could be lit to warn troops along the Great Wall of impending danger. During the rule of the Ming dynasty, which controlled China from 1368 to 1644, the Great Wall was rebuilt in the form in which it survives today.

BUILDER'S MARK

The inscription on this brick records that it was made in the twelfth year of the reign of the Ming Emperor Wan Li, which was 1585. The Ming dynasty's efforts to strengthen the Great Wall did not prevent an invasion by the Manchus, who took over China in 1644.

BUILDING THE WALL

The Great Wall was built by slaves working in terrible conditions, supervised by soldiers. Much of it passes through desert, and sandstorms often interrupted the work. Temporary walls had to be built to keep sand out of the foundations. Food supplies often ran short when bandits attacked the supply wagons, but the slaves were forced to work on. If they fell ill they were simply thrown into the foundations of the Great Wall and building continued over their bodies. The same fate awaited anyone who made a mistake or failed to work hard enough.

FROM MOUNTAINS TO SEA

The Great Wall's western end is at Yumen, high in the mountains of northwest China. It follows the hilltops and high ground, giving the troops who manned it a commanding view. The Great Wall finishes almost 2,000 kilometres away at Shanhaiguan on the Gulf of Bo Hai, an inlet of the Pacific Ocean. The spine of the Great Wall has a series of branches striking off to the south, marking the efforts of successive rulers to defend their borders.

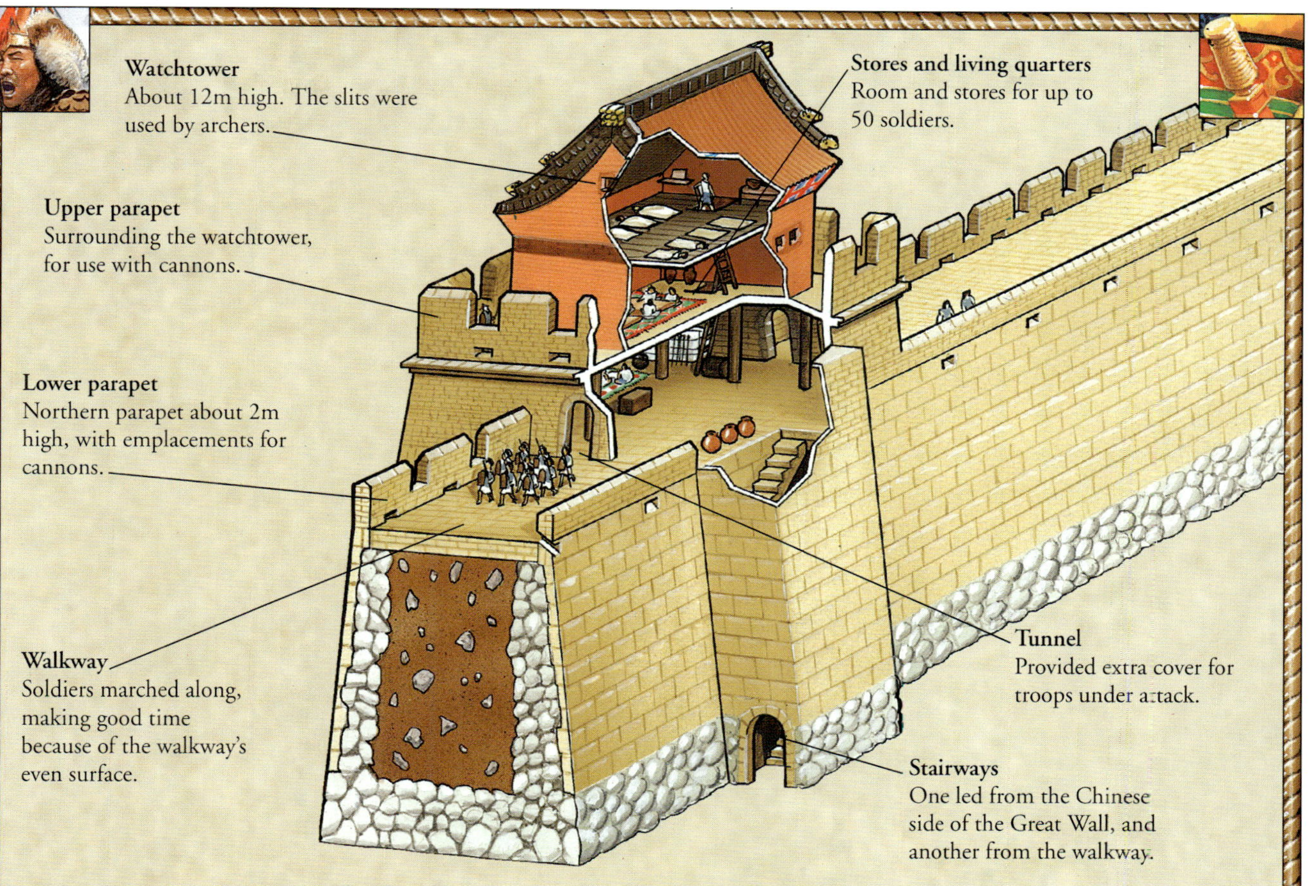

The Great Wall is between 7m and 8m high, roughly the same width at the base, tapering to about 5m at the top. It was built on a stone foundation 1.5m thick.

ATTACK!

Most of the time the Great Wall formed an effective defence against disorganised bands of raiders, who were outnumbered and easily fought off. But in the thirteenth century a ferocious and efficient army under the Mongol Emperor Genghis Khan breached the Great Wall with battering rams, heavy catapults and gunpowder. Genghis Khan's army of 250,000 horsemen was famous for its cruelty – all enemy prisoners were killed – and its determination to win. The Mongols swept on to conquer China, and stayed for nearly a hundred years. After the Mongols were finally driven out, the emperors of the Ming dynasty rebuilt and strengthened the existing Great Wall, and extended it.

FIRST EMPEROR

Qin Shih Huang Ti (259–210 BC) was the first emperor to rule over the whole of China. It was during his reign that the short lengths of earth wall that already existed were rebuilt and incorporated into a new continuous stone wall. The Great Wall became a symbol of the unity of the new China under Emperor Shih. When he died, he was buried in a huge tomb with a "terracotta army" of 7,500 life-sized model soldiers to guard him. These models were not seen again until 1974, when the tomb was discovered near Xi'an.

Colosseum

"Hail, Caesar, those who are about to die salute you."
The gladiators' greeting to the emperor, AD 80–523

GLADIATOR'S HELMET

A heavily armoured gladiator was called a murmillo. He wore a metal helmet with a sturdy ridge along the top to protect his skull from blows. It also had a grille at the front, which protected his face but gave him less good vision than his opponent.

The ruins of the Colosseum in Rome still stand – despite many fires, earthquakes and military attacks – as a reminder of the great days of the Roman Empire nearly 2,000 years ago. The huge oval amphitheatre, which was completed in AD 80, could seat up to 50,000 people. It was used for a variety of spectacular entertainments, including gladiator contests, chariot races and even a mock sea battle, for which the whole arena had to be flooded.

The name Colosseum comes from the Latin word *colosseus*, meaning "gigantic". It probably refers to the amphitheatre's vast size, as well as to the colossal statue of the Emperor Nero that stood nearby. The foundations were made from concrete and the huge main structure from stone, with four levels of columns on the outside. Inside, the seats were tiered so that everyone had a good view of the arena. Underneath the wooden floor of the arena was a vast network of passages, with dens for the wild animals and rooms for the gladiators and other performers.

ARMED COMBAT

Gladiators were usually slaves captured in war. They were trained to fight to the death. The various types fought each other using different kinds of weapons. A retiarius gladiator carried a three-pronged spear and used a net to trap his heavily armoured opponent, a murmillo gladiator.

BUILDING THE AMPHITHEATRE

The Colosseum took a large workforce of slaves over 10 years to build. It was started in AD 70 by the Emperor Vespasian, but he died a year before it was finished. It was completed and opened by his son Titus in AD 80. Two years later the Emperor Domitian added a fourth storey.

RAISING THE ROOF

The Colosseum's sun canopy was probably raised from the floor of the arena using ropes. It was hauled up using 80 sets of pulleys and winches installed at the top of the building.

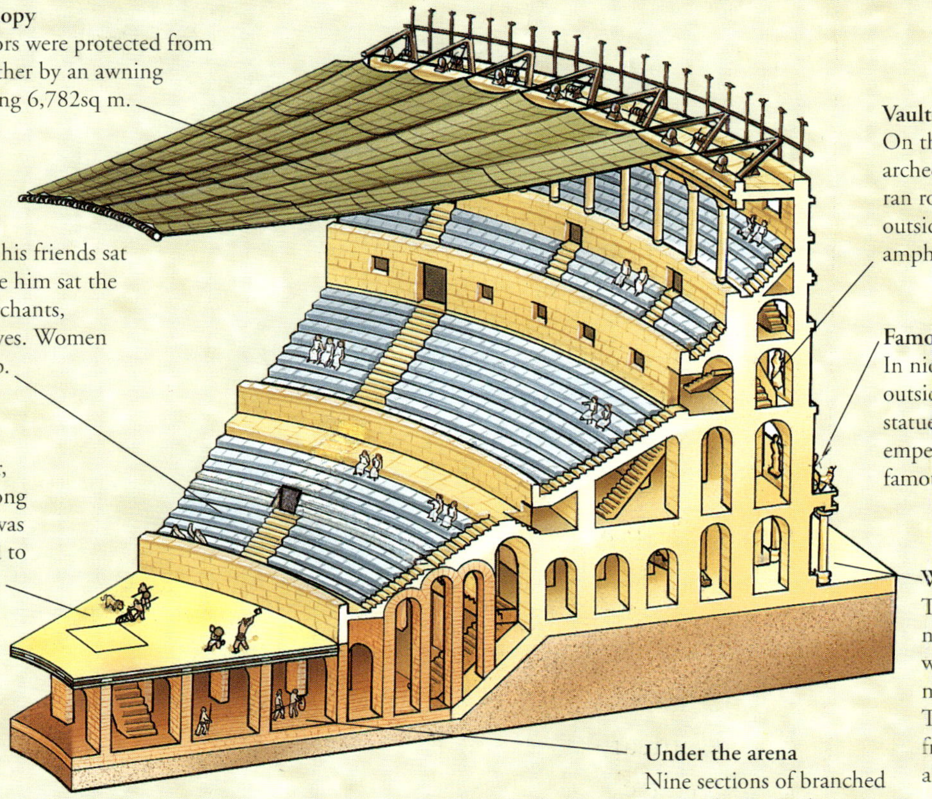

The Colosseum measures 187m across at its widest point, and was almost 50m tall. It was badly damaged by an earthquake in 1231.

ANIMAL SLAUGHTER

The killing of wild animals by gladiators was a popular sport. On the Colosseum's opening day, some 5,000 animals were slaughtered. They included lions, tigers, elephants and leopards. The animals were brought up from below the arena in a cage balanced with a counterweight, and they were released through trap doors for their final fight. Criminals were also killed by being hurled into the arena to be eaten by lions.

Anderton Boat Lift

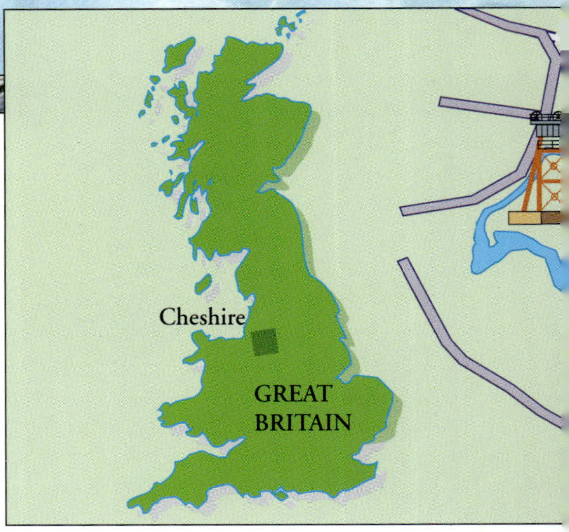

"*The Anderton Boat Lift is one of the seven wonders of British waterways.*"
Robert Aickmann *The Story of Our Inland Waterways* 1955

There are three ways of enabling canal and river boats to change levels. The most common method is to use a lock, in which the water level is raised or lowered to move a boat from one level to another. The second way is to haul a boat over rollers. The third is to use a vertical lift. The Anderton Boat Lift in northwest England is the only surviving example of a vertical lift in Britain. It is one of only eight such lifts in the world. Although it is no longer used, there are plans to restore it.

The Lift carried boats between the River Weaver, and the Trent and Mersey Canal over 15 metres above. When it first opened in 1875 it was operated hydraulically, but it became unsafe and in 1908 a new Lift, described here, was installed. This Lift worked in a simple, but ingenious way. Cast-iron weights balanced the weight of the tanks and meant that gravity provided most of the power. A small electric motor provided the rest.

PULLEY SYSTEM

Each boat-carrying tank was suspended on wires that ran from the tank over pulleys down to a set of cast-iron weights. These were equal to the weight of the water-filled tank. The tank was raised or lowered by turning the pulleys one way or the other.

SALT CHUTES

There were three large salt works near the site of the Boat Lift. Traffic on the River Weaver depended on exporting their salt and importing coal and china clay. Salt from the canal boats at the top of the Lift was poured down chutes to the river barges waiting below.

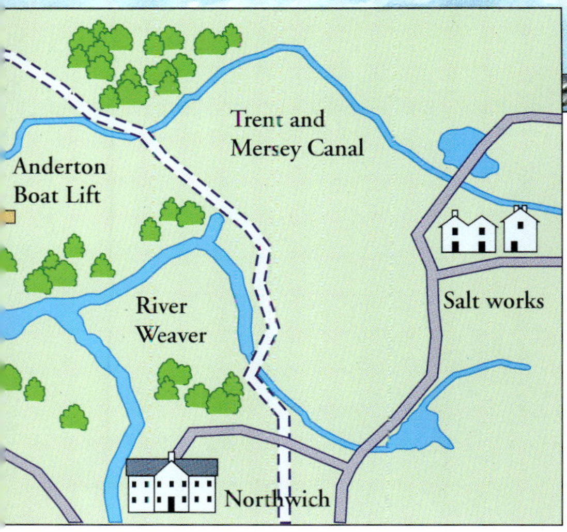

CANAL JUNCTION

The Boat Lift is sited at the village of Anderton, in Cheshire, at a junction in Britain's inland waterway system. The River Weaver was navigable from the sea to this point, and the Trent and Mersey Canal ran close to it, but at a higher level. The Lift was built to avoid having to transfer cargoes overland between the two waterways.

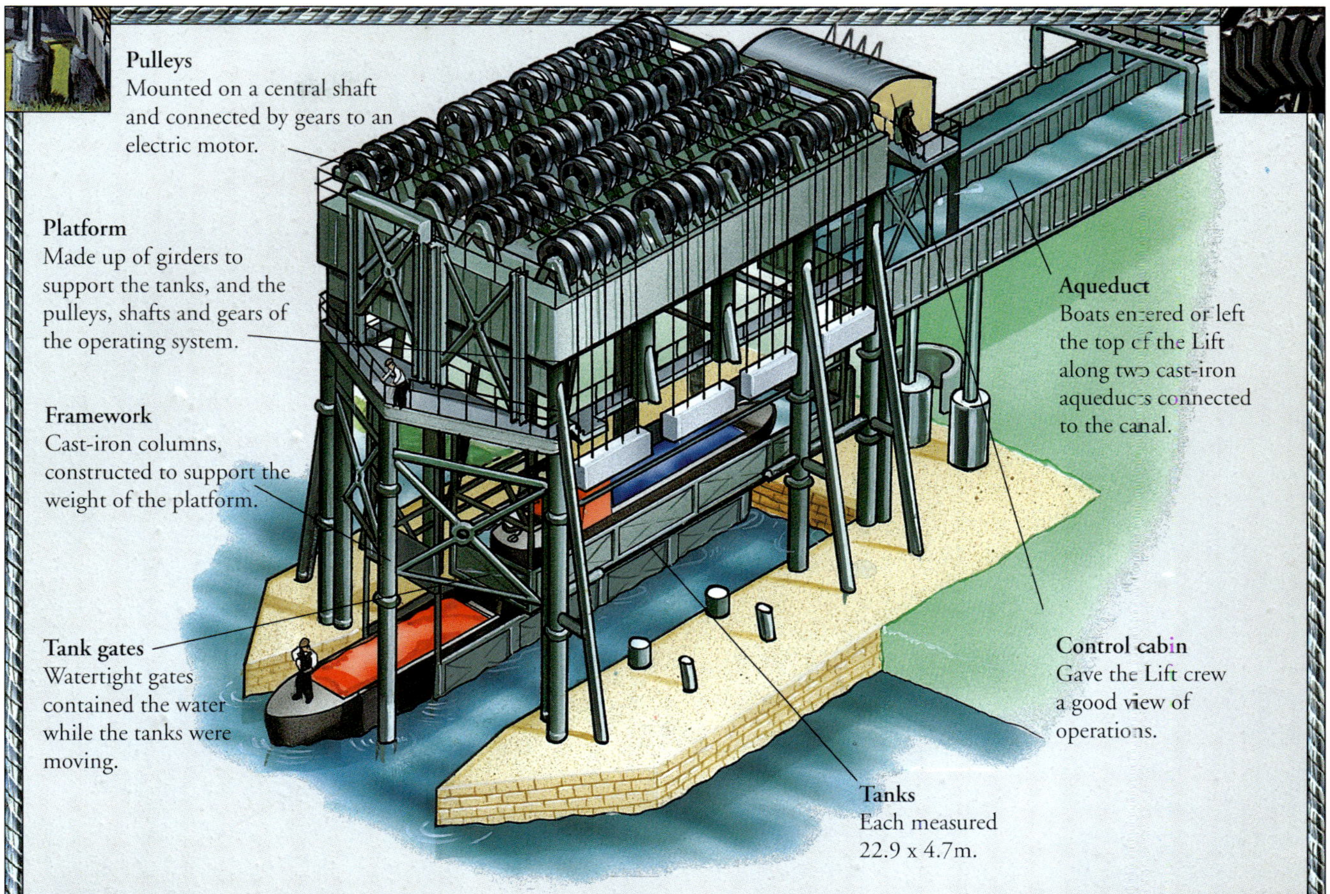

The Anderton Boat Lift raised and lowered boats 15.3m between the two water levels. The Lift was powered by a 30hp motor. When full, each tank weighed about 252 tonnes.

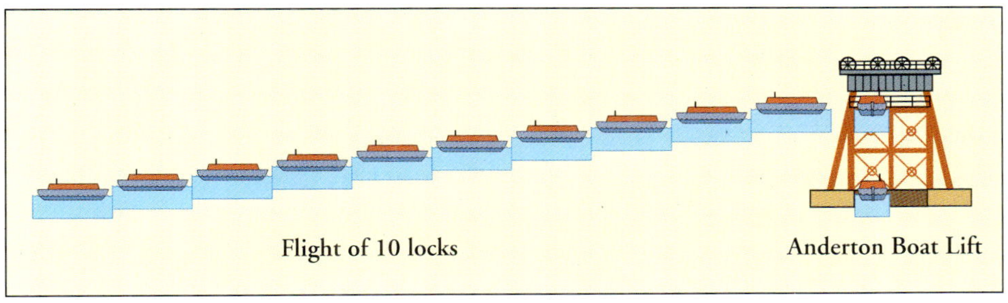

LOCKS VERSUS LIFT

A series of locks to carry traffic between the River Weaver and the Trent and Mersey Canal would have taken far more space than was available. A flight of 10 locks would have been needed. The Lift provided a much faster, more efficient way of connecting the two waterways.

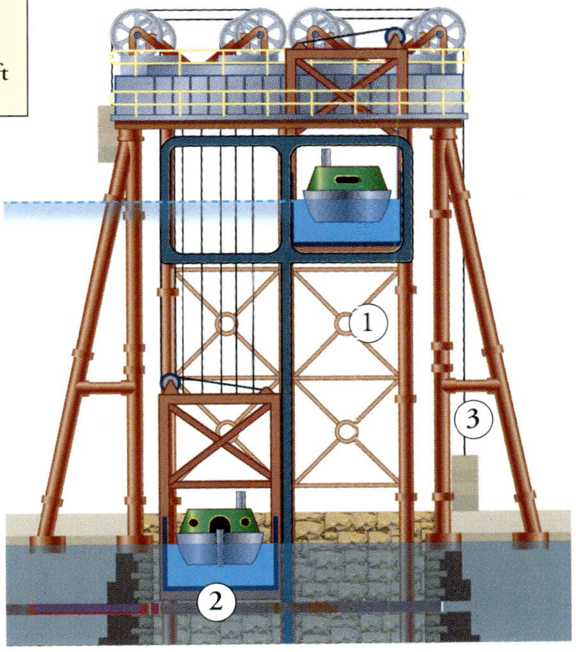

PULLEY POWER

The second Lift was built over the top of the original Victorian structure. Tubular cast-iron columns formed the framework (1). These had to be strong enough to take the weight of two water-filled tanks (2) and their counterweights (3). Each tank was counterbalanced by its own set of weights so that it could be operated independently. Operations at the lower, river end were controlled from a cabin at the foot of the Lift, and this was connected by a signalling system to the main control room at the top.

TWO-WAY TRAFFIC

Two aqueducts allowed traffic to pass to and from the Lift and the Trent and Mersey Canal. They were long enough, at 50 metres, to allow boats to wait for the Lift without holding up traffic on the canal. There were docks at the top where boats could take on cargo and supplies.

Statue of Liberty

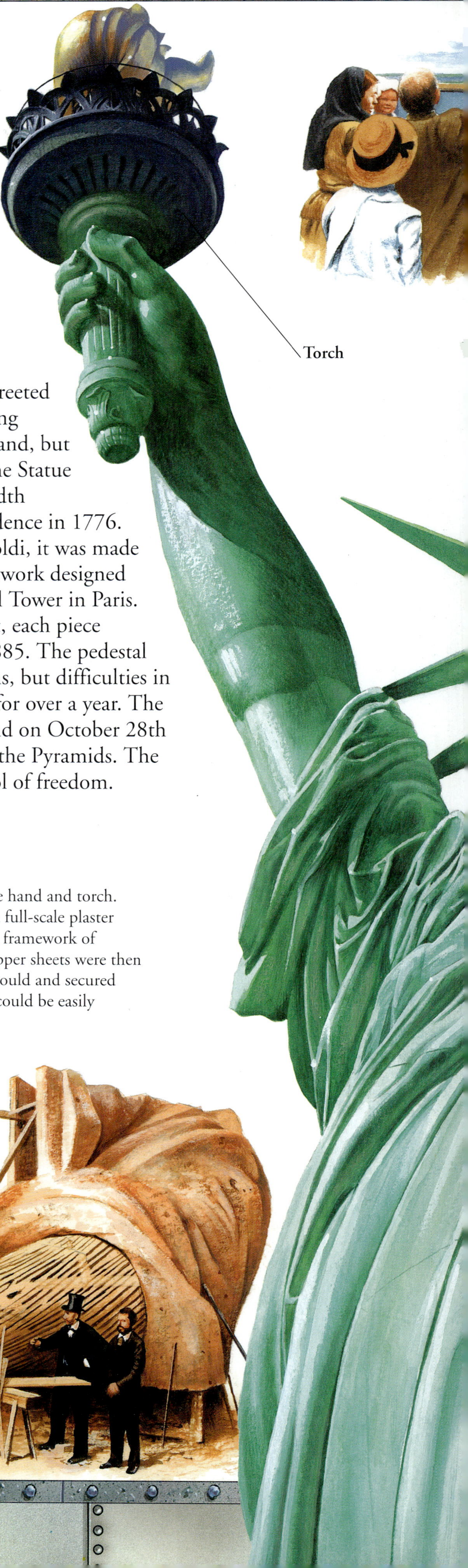

"Here at our sea-washed, sunset gates shall stand
A mighty woman with a torch, whose flame
Is the imprisoned lightning, and her name
Mother of Exiles."
Emma Lazarus *The New Colossus* 1883

Travellers arriving by boat at New York Harbour are greeted by the magnificent sight of the Statue of Liberty, rising 91.5 metres above the water. Liberty stands on a small island, but from a distance she seems to be rising from the waves. The Statue was a gift from the people of France, to mark the hundredth anniversary of the United States' Declaration of Independence in 1776. The work of the French sculptor Frédéric Auguste Bartholdi, it was made from sheets of beaten copper fixed to a central iron framework designed by Alexandre Gustave Eiffel, who later designed the Eiffel Tower in Paris. The Statue was assembled in France and then taken apart, each piece carefully numbered, for the sea voyage to New York in 1885. The pedestal on which Liberty stands was paid for by American citizens, but difficulties in raising the money delayed the completion of the project for over a year. The Statue was finally dedicated by President Grover Cleveland on October 28th 1886. It was the tallest structure to have been built since the Pyramids. The Statue has now stood for over a hundred years as a symbol of freedom.

LIBERTY'S TABLET

July 4th 1776, written in Roman numerals on the Statue's tablet, was the date when the United States of America issued its Declaration of Independence from Britain. War had already broken out between British and American forces, and fighting was to last until 1781. The Americans were aided by France.

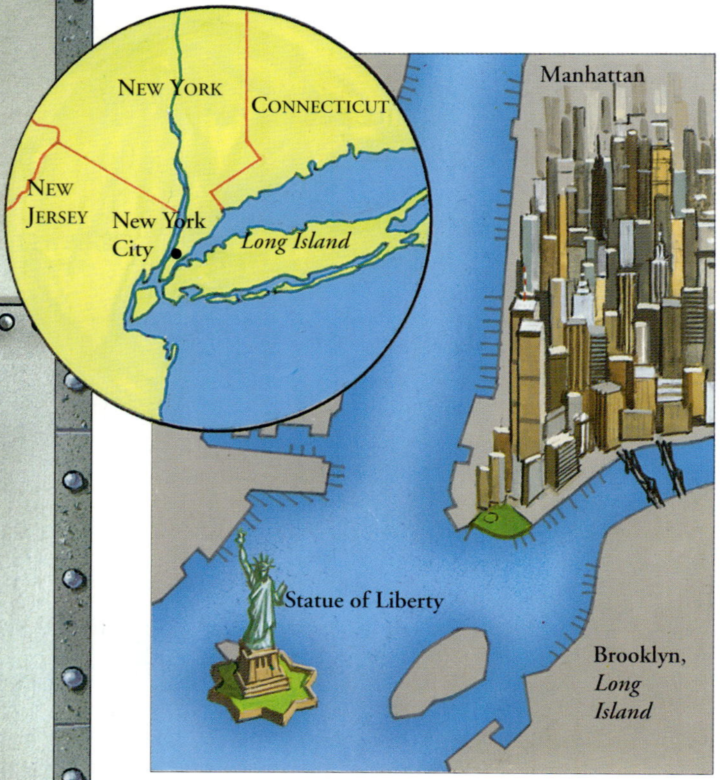

LIBERTY ISLAND

The island on which the Statue of Liberty stands was formerly called Bedloe's Island. It was the site of a fort that commanded the entrance to the port of New York. It was renamed Liberty Island in 1956. From 1892 to 1954, people coming to live in the United States passed through an immigration centre on nearby Ellis Island.

BUILDING THE STATUE

The first sections to be made were the hand and torch. From a one-third-scale clay model a full-scale plaster copy was made. This was covered with a framework of wooden slats to make a mould. Thin copper sheets were then beaten into shape around the wooden mould and secured with one rivet in ten, so that the Statue could be easily dismantled for shipping to America.

NEW AMERICANS

Between 1870 and 1910, over 18 million immigrants arrived in the United States from Europe, fleeing poverty and persecution. They included millions of Russian and Polish Jews who were driven out of their own countries. From 1886 onwards, the Statue of Liberty welcomed them to their new lives of freedom.

The Statue itself is 45.3m high, and the pedestal is 46.2m. The Statue weighs almost 204 tonnes. The pedestal's concrete foundation used 24,000 barrels of Portland cement.

HELP AT HAND

Liberty has suffered badly from corrosion. A chemical reaction between the iron rods and the copper skin caused the rods to swell up and rivets to break off, weakening the structure. In a major restoration project of the 1980s, every iron rod had to be replaced with new ones made from stainless steel.

Eiffel Tower

"Just because we are engineers does not necessarily mean that we give no thought to beauty in our constructions, or that in making something solid and long-lasting we ignore elegance."
A.G. Eiffel, replying to criticism of his Tower, 1887

When the Paris Exhibition of 1889 was being planned to celebrate the centenary of the French Revolution, the organisers held a competition for the best design of a tower to act as a focal point. There were over a hundred contestants, and the winning design was by Alexandre Gustave Eiffel.

Construction began on January 29th 1887 and was completed just over two years later. The Eiffel Tower's 12,000 iron parts were factory-made, drilled for rivets and numbered, before being brought to the site for assembly. Eiffel was an engineer rather than an architect, and his design reflected the latest engineering technology of his day. The Tower was originally 300 metres high, but in 1957 television aerials were added, raising the height to 318.7 metres. During its construction the Tower aroused fierce controversy. A group of artists and writers described it in a Paris newspaper as "a dizzily ridiculous tower dominating Paris like a huge, black factory chimney". But it was a great success with tourists, and nearly two million people visited it in the first five months after it opened.

LIGHT SHOW

From 1925 to 1936, the French car-maker Citroën sponsored a display of lights, using 250,000 coloured bulbs, on the Eiffel Tower. The Citroën name could be seen shining from three sides of the Tower up to 38 kilometres away.

GOING UP

Five hydraulic lifts, like the one above, were originally fitted. Four went up to the first and second floors, and the fifth took visitors from the second floor to the top. Today, two hydraulic and two electric lifts travel to the first and second floors. Two more lifts take visitors on up to the third floor.

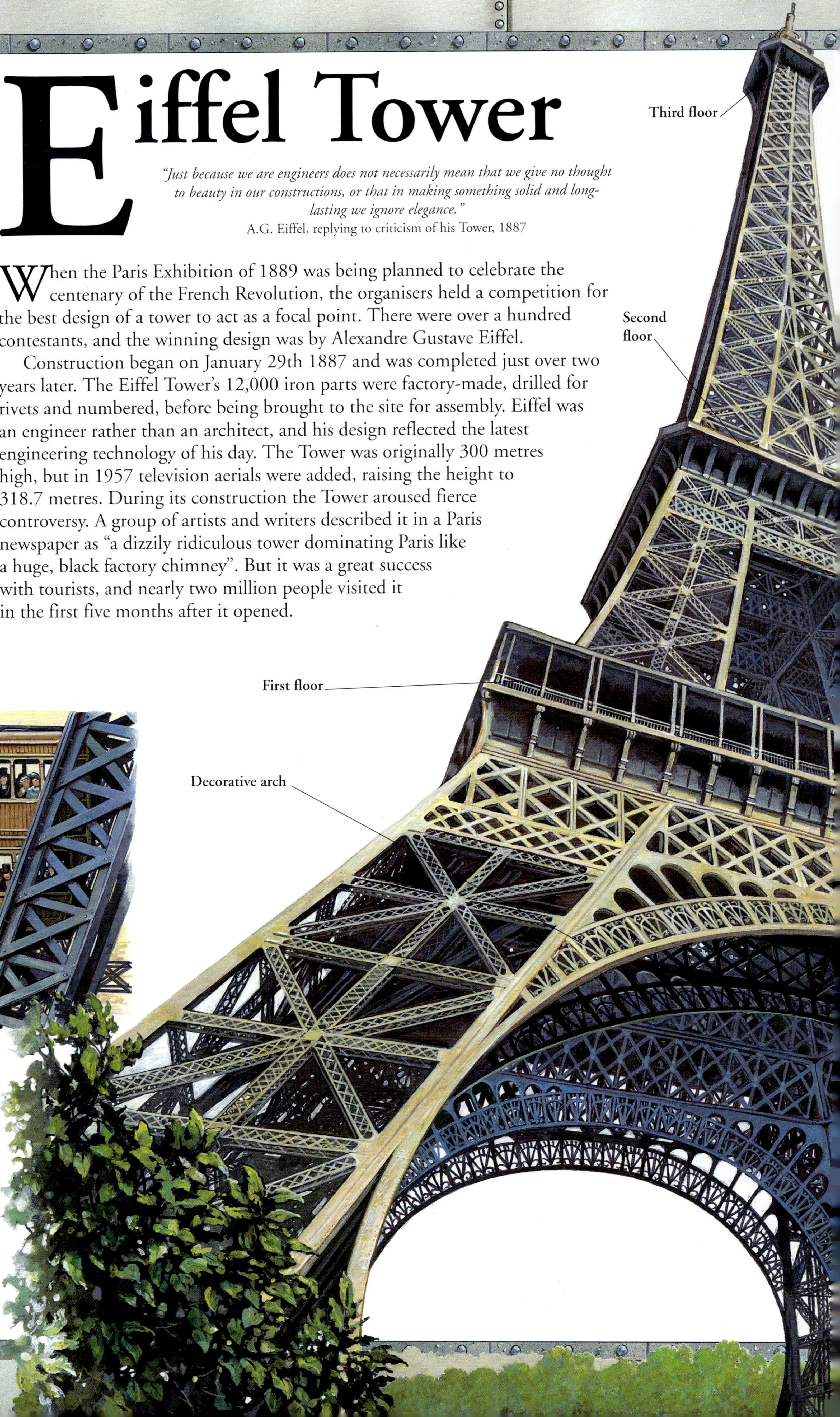

ROOFTOPS OF PARIS

The top of the Eiffel Tower gives a fine view over Paris. But lifts were not installed in time for the opening ceremony in March 1889, and guests had to climb to the top up a 911-step spiral staircase, since removed. Not all of them made it, but Eiffel did, and proudly hoisted the French flag from the top.

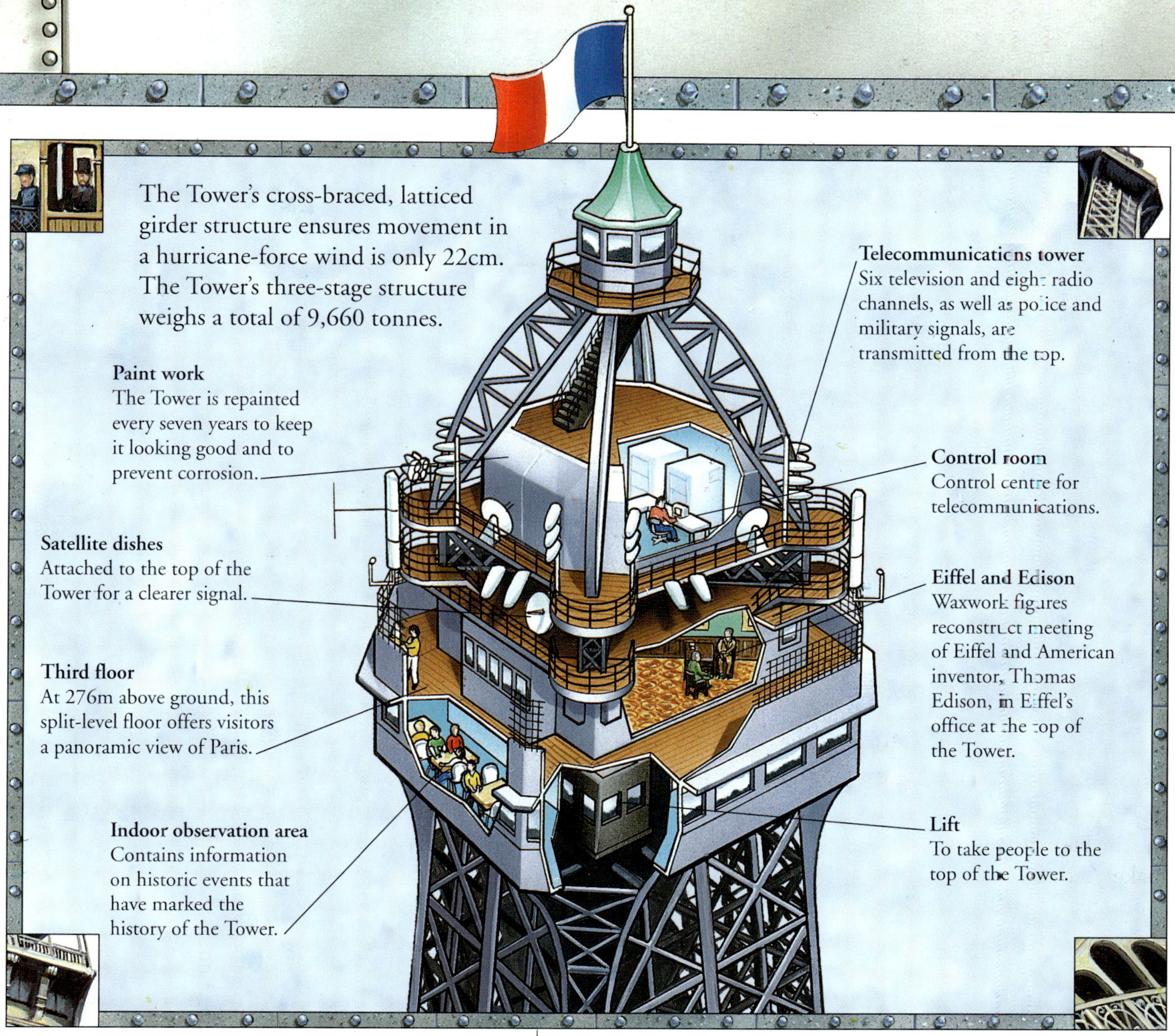

STAGE BY STAGE

The Tower was built in stages, each floor in turn providing a working surface for the floor above. The lift tracks were fitted as work proceeded, and were used to carry cranes. The foundations were finished in June 1887 and by November the legs were well under way (1). The first floor (2) was completed on April 1st 1888, the second floor (3) on August 14th, and the third floor (4) by December in the same year. The top of the Tower (5) was completed on March 31st 1889.

ELEPHANT WALK

The Eiffel Tower, in its history of over a century, has been the scene of many famous stunts. Daredevil human visitors have included parachutists, trick-cyclists and tightrope walkers. In 1948, the oldest female elephant in the world, aged 85, was taken for a long, slow walk up as far as the first floor by her owner.

Empire State Building

"The Empire State Building stands today as the greatest monument to ingenuity, to skill, to brain power, to muscle power, the tallest thing in the world today produced by the hand of man."
Alfred E. Smith, opening the Empire State Building in 1931

On August 29th 1929, New York newspapers reported plans for a new building on Fifth Avenue in the heart of Manhattan. Work was to start on the Empire State Building, planned to be 381 metres high, with 102 storeys. It would be the tallest building in the world. Constructing a building of this size on a restricted site amid the bustle of New York's business district posed huge challenges. But the workmen laboured around the clock – they even ate on the job – and the Empire State Building was opened on May 1st 1931. It had been built in just 15 months.

The Empire State Building is more than an office block. It is a major tourist attraction. Visitors can take an express lift to the observatory on the 86th floor, which welcomes thousands of tourists a day. There is another observation platform on the 102nd floor. The Empire State Building held its title of the tallest skyscraper in the world until 1973, when it was overtaken by the twin towers of the World Trade Center – 31 metres taller – in Manhattan.

FILM STARDOM

Almost as soon as it was built, the Empire State Building became a film star. In the 1933 fantasy film *King Kong*, the giant ape fought on top of the building against US Army Air Force fighters before he was shot down.

AIRSHIP MAST

At the time the skyscraper was designed, airships seemed the most likely means of long-distance air travel, so a mooring mast for airships was fixed to the top of the Building. But high winds made mooring too dangerous, and the scheme was abandoned. The mast became instead a housing for telecommunications antennae.

MEN AT WORK

The riveting gangs put together the steel frame at a furious pace. The casual way they rode the girders without hard hats or safety harnesses would not be allowed today!

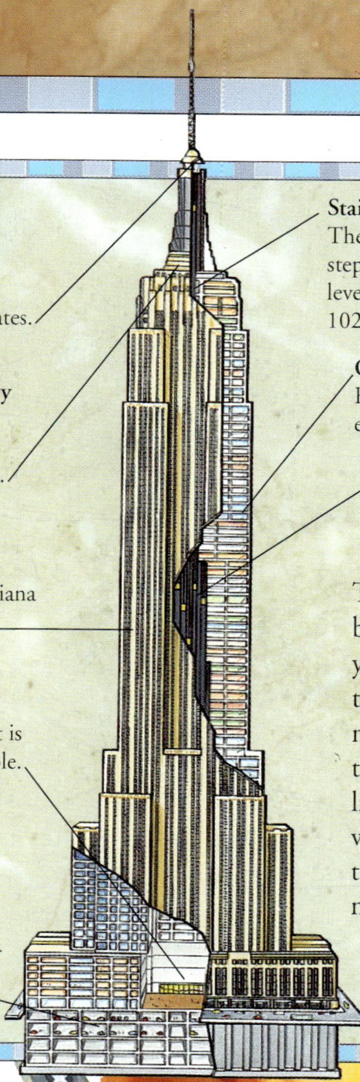

The steel-framed building took one year and 45 days to complete, and measures 443.2m to the top of the lightning rod. It weighs 308,000 tonnes. Visitors number over 2.5 million each year.

EMERGENCY!

On July 28th 1945, a nightmare came true. An aircraft crashed at full speed into the Empire State Building, causing $1 million worth of damage. It was a B-25 bomber with a crew of two; both men were killed. Another 12 people inside the building died. If it had not been a Saturday the death-toll would have been much higher. The causes were never explained.

WORLD'S TALLEST BUILDINGS

The tallest office buildings without a mast are the Petronas Towers in Kuala Lumpur. But taller still because of their masts are the Ostankino TV Tower in Moscow at 537m and the CN Tower in Toronto at 553m. The topmost 100m of each is a transmission mast.

1. Eiffel Tower, Paris (1889), 300m.
2. Chrysler Building, New York (1930), 319m.
3. John Hancock Center, Chicago (1968), 343m.
4. Empire State Building, New York (1931), 381m.
5. Sears Tower, Chicago (1974), 443m.
6. Petronas Towers, Kuala Lumpur (1996), 452m.

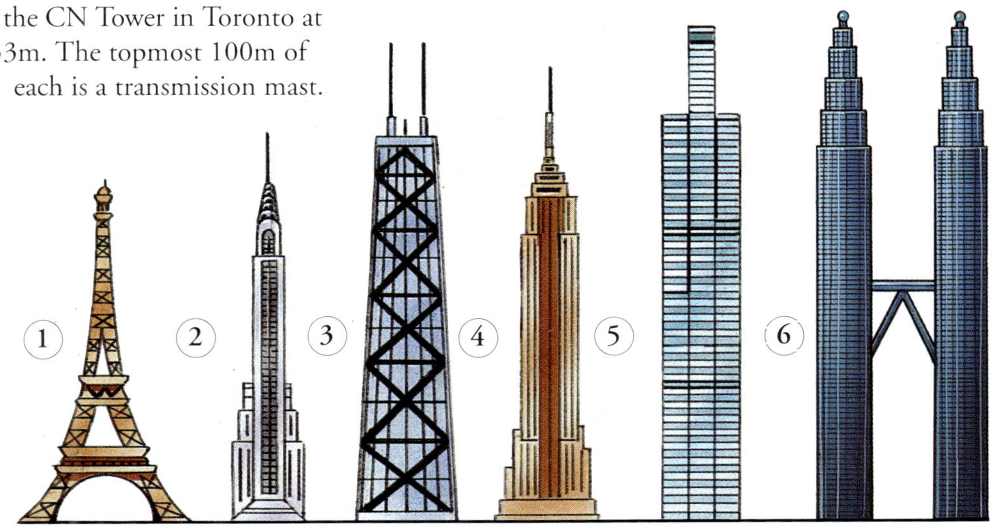

Sydney Harbour Bridge

"Constructed in the cantilever method with the half-arches held back by steel cables, [it] is undoubtedly the most celebrated and most massive bridge of its kind."
David J. Brown, Editor, Ove Arup Journal, 1993

MEETING POINT

The moment came in September 1930 when the two halves of the arch met in the middle. Onshore cables supporting the two halves were slackened off slowly so that the pieces sank into place against each other.

This giant steel-arch bridge is so wide it carries eight road lanes, two railway tracks, a cycle track and a pedestrian walkway across Australia's Sydney Harbour from Dawes Point to Milson Point. At 48.8 metres wide, it is the broadest long-span bridge in the world. The deck of the Bridge is supported by steel cables, called hangers, suspended from an arch of steel girders and plates. All the steel components were made in Britain and assembled in workshops near the Bridge site. The sections were floated into position on the water and then lifted into place by cranes standing on the growing arch. The Bridge was designed to give 52 metres' headroom to ships passing beneath it.

Design work began in 1923, building started in 1927, and the Bridge was opened for traffic in 1932. To answer any public concerns about its safety, 72 railway locomotives weighing a total of almost 550,000 tonnes were shunted on to the Bridge while structural checks were carried out.

DANGEROUS WORK

Labourers worked high above the water with few safety precautions. They had no protective clothing or helmets, and no guardrail either. Several men died during the Bridge's construction.

CROSSING THE WATER

Steel cables supported the two halves of the Bridge as they were built towards each other (1). The cables also had to support the weight of the cranes that lifted the arch sections into position (2). When the arch was complete, the steel hangers were lowered into place (3), followed by the sections of the deck (4).

NATURAL HARBOUR

Sydney is Australia's largest city and chief port, and capital of the state of New South Wales. This bustling city of 3,699,000 people stands beside one of the world's great natural harbours. The Harbour Bridge was built as part of a programme to improve the city's communications without harming its shipping trade.

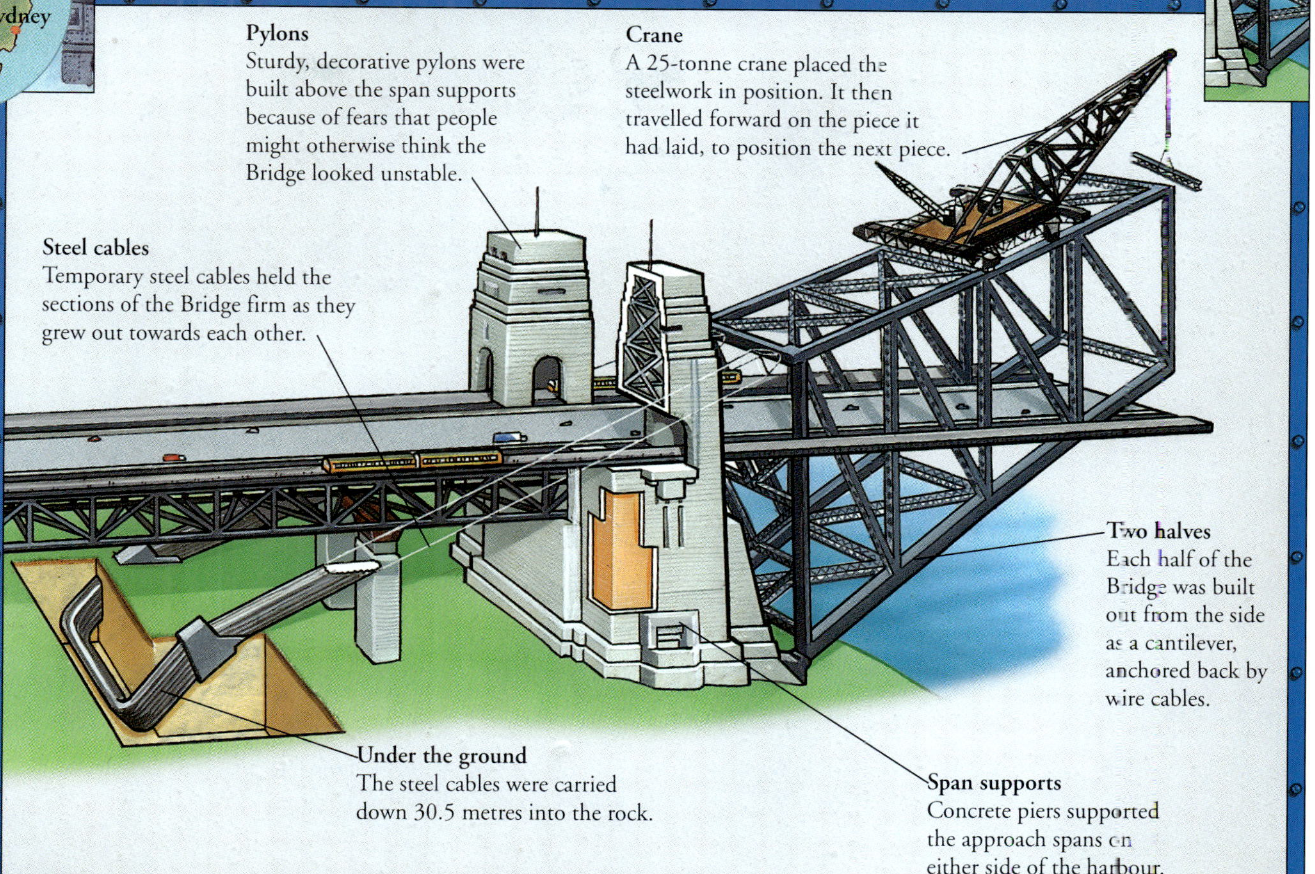

Sydney Harbour Bridge measures 509m long and 48.8m wide. Its single steel arch weighs 28,000 tonnes.

BRIDGE TYPES

There are several types of bridge construction. These include a suspension bridge, which hangs from cables that run over the tops of towers (1); a cantilever bridge, built out in sections, with each section fixed at one end (2); and a steel-arch bridge (3), such as Sydney Harbour Bridge.

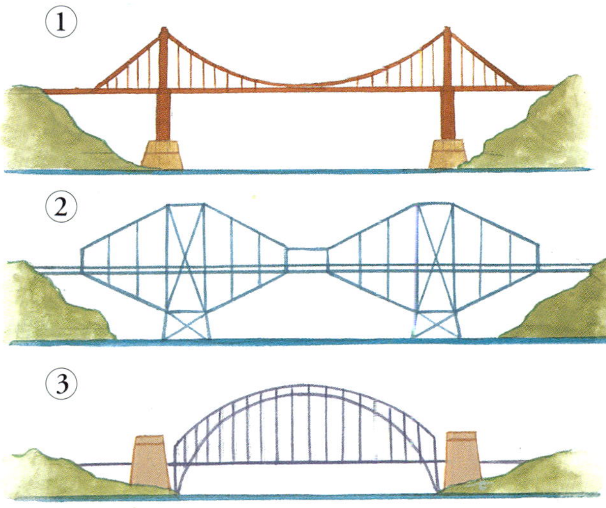

VLA Radio Telescope

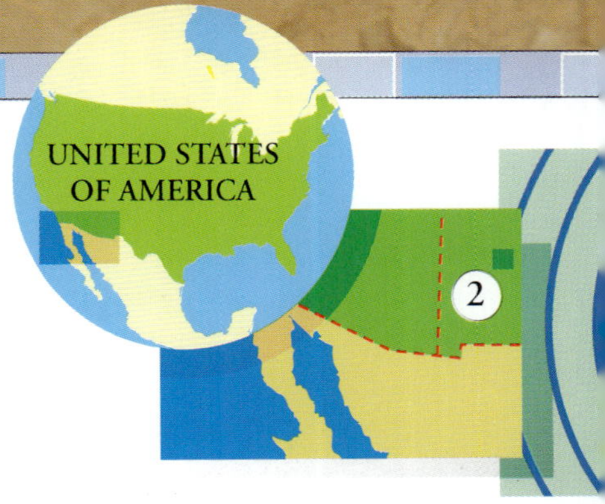

From a site on the plains of New Mexico, USA, 27 large metal dishes continuously sweep space for signals from the stars. The dishes make up the VLA (Very Large Array) Radio Telescope operated by the United States National Science Foundation. Unlike optical telescopes that give a visual image, radio telescopes pick up radio waves sent out by objects in space. Many of these objects are too distant to be seen with an optical telescope. The weak radio signals are amplified and recorded so that they can be studied by astronomers. Since about 1960, radio astronomy has transformed scientific ideas about the nature and size of the universe.

The VLA Radio Telescope was opened in 1980. Its metal dishes, which all focus on the same object, are arranged in the shape of a Y. They are connected electronically so that their signals can be combined. The effect is the same as one huge dish 27 kilometres in diameter.

"The great radio telescopes and optical telescopes have discovered objects of a type unknown only a few years ago. Some of these lie in the remote parts of space and time and convey to us on Earth records of the early history of the universe."

Sir Bernard Lovell, pioneer radio astronomer, 1974

SUBREFLECTOR

The purpose of the subreflector is to collect radio waves bounced off the parabolic dish and focus them. This provides a signal strong enough for the receiver to amplify and interpret. A strong signal is needed to overcome the problem of radio noise – interference from other objects in space or from radios and televisions.

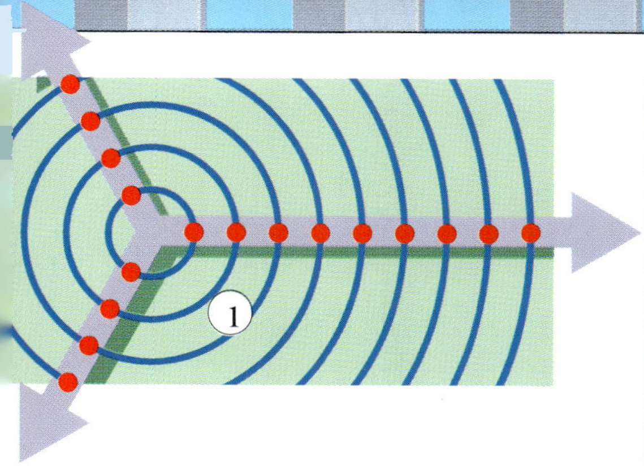

VLA SITE

The VLA site (1) is 80 kilometres west of Socorro, on the Plains of San Augustin (2) in southern New Mexico. The site was chosen carefully. It is far enough south to enable radio astronomers to study 85 per cent of the sky both north and south of the equator. On the flat desert ground, it is easy to make full use of the mobility of each dish.

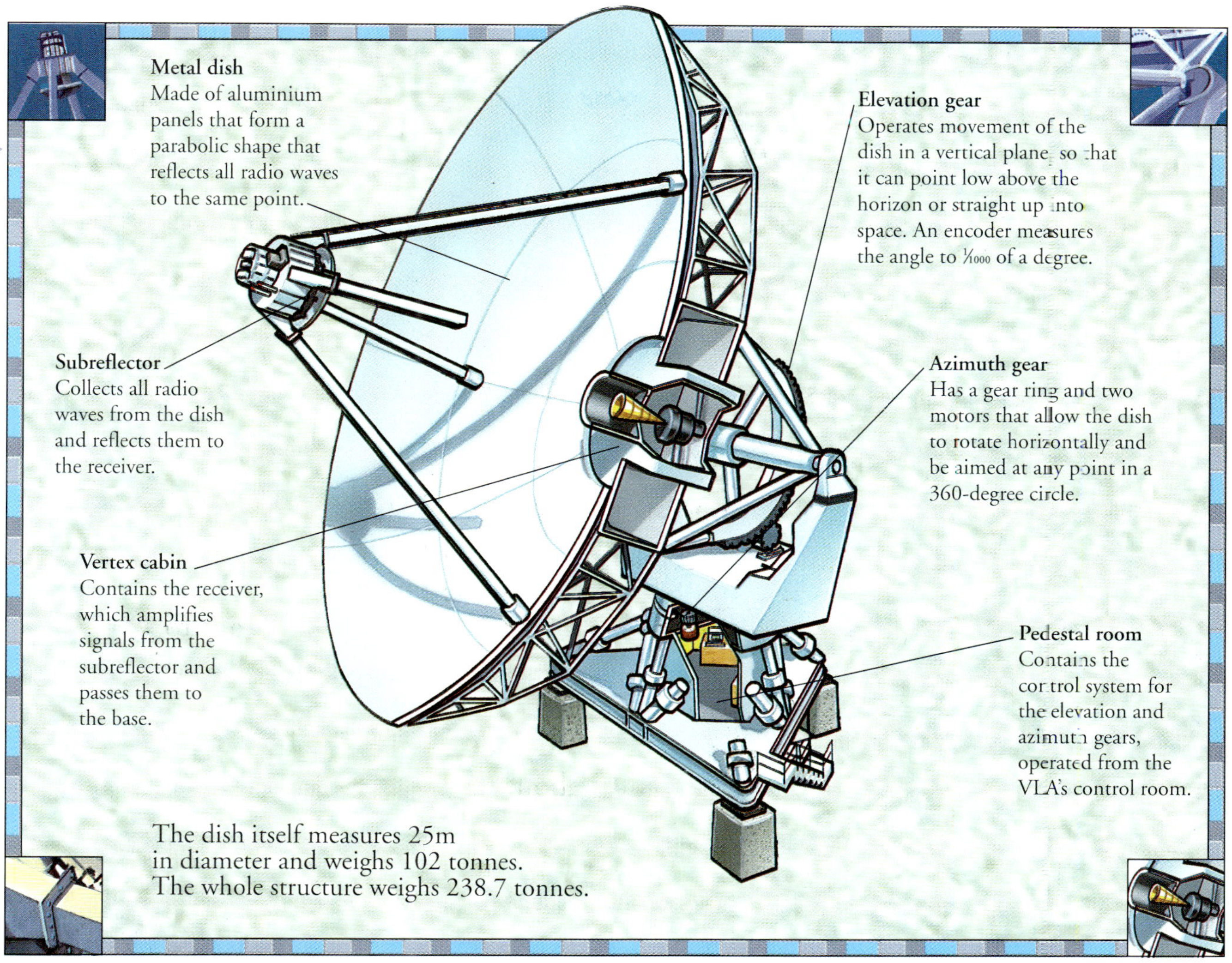

The dish itself measures 25m in diameter and weighs 102 tonnes. The whole structure weighs 238.7 tonnes.

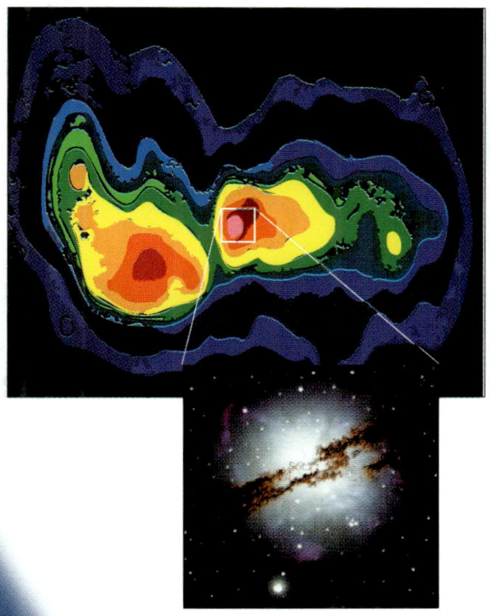

Centaurus A

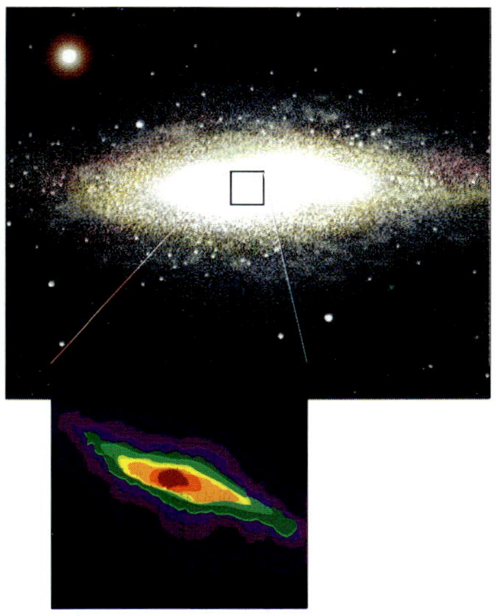

M 82

COLLECTING WAVES

Radio signals have to be collected over a large area and brought into focus. The parallel radio waves bounce off the bowl-shaped dish (1) to a subreflector (2). From there, the waves are reflected again to the receiver (3), which amplifies them and converts them into electrical signals.

RADIO MAPS

Signals received by the VLA's dishes are used to build up maps of distant galaxies. In some cases a radio telescope can detect features that are much more extensive than the part seen through an optical telescope. This is the case with the galaxy Centaurus A. Only a small part of it – partly obscured by dust – is visible through an optical telescope (bottom left). The radio map (top left) covers a much wider area and gives a more accurate picture of the galaxy. With the galaxy M 82, the optical image (top right) is larger than the radio source. The radio waves come from the central part of the galaxy. This indicates that a hydrogen gas outburst took place one to two million years before our present view of the galaxy, which is 8.5 million light-years away.

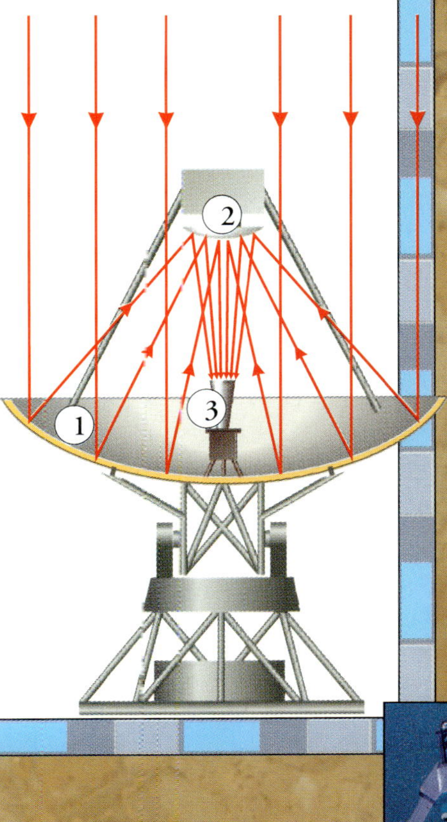

NASA Shuttle launch site

"The general reliability and versatility which the Shuttle offers seem likely to establish it quickly as the workhorse of our whole space effort."
President Richard Nixon, announcing the Shuttle programme in 1972

INTO SPACE

The United States' space programme is controlled by the National Aeronautics and Space Administration (NASA). Its duties include organising manned spaceflights, orbital satellites and unmanned space probes to the planets.

The Space Shuttle is a rocket-powered spacecraft designed to return to Earth after each mission and be re-used. The United States launched its first Shuttle in 1981, from the Kennedy Space Center at Cape Canaveral in Florida. In the next ten years, another 37 Shuttle missions lifted off from the same launch complex. The Shuttle is made up of three parts. The crew and their cargo travel into space in an orbiter. This rides on a huge external fuel tank that detaches after take-off and burns up as it re-enters the atmosphere. Two solid-fuel rocket boosters also drop away after use and parachute to Earth, to be recovered and re-used.

The launch site also contains a huge vehicle assembly building where the Shuttle parts are put together. A control centre is on site, together with design and testing facilities, and a 4,572-metre-long landing runway.

CRAWLER-TRANSPORTER

A giant crawler-transporter, moving at no more than 1.6 kilometres per hour, carries the Shuttle over 5 kilometres from the assembly building to the launch pad. The crawler-transporter moves on eight caterpillar tracks, each one over 3 metres high. It travels on a specially built road surface that sinks as the transporter passes over it, but springs back into place afterwards.

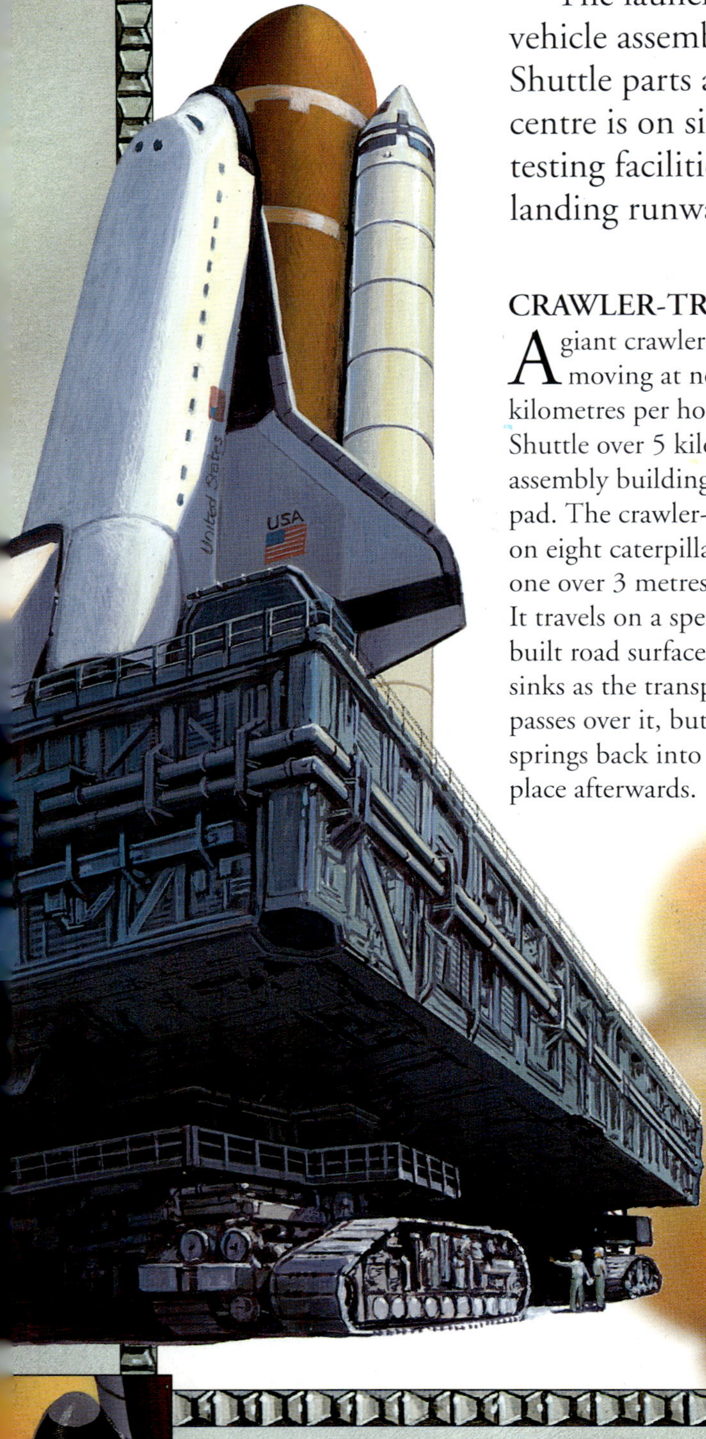

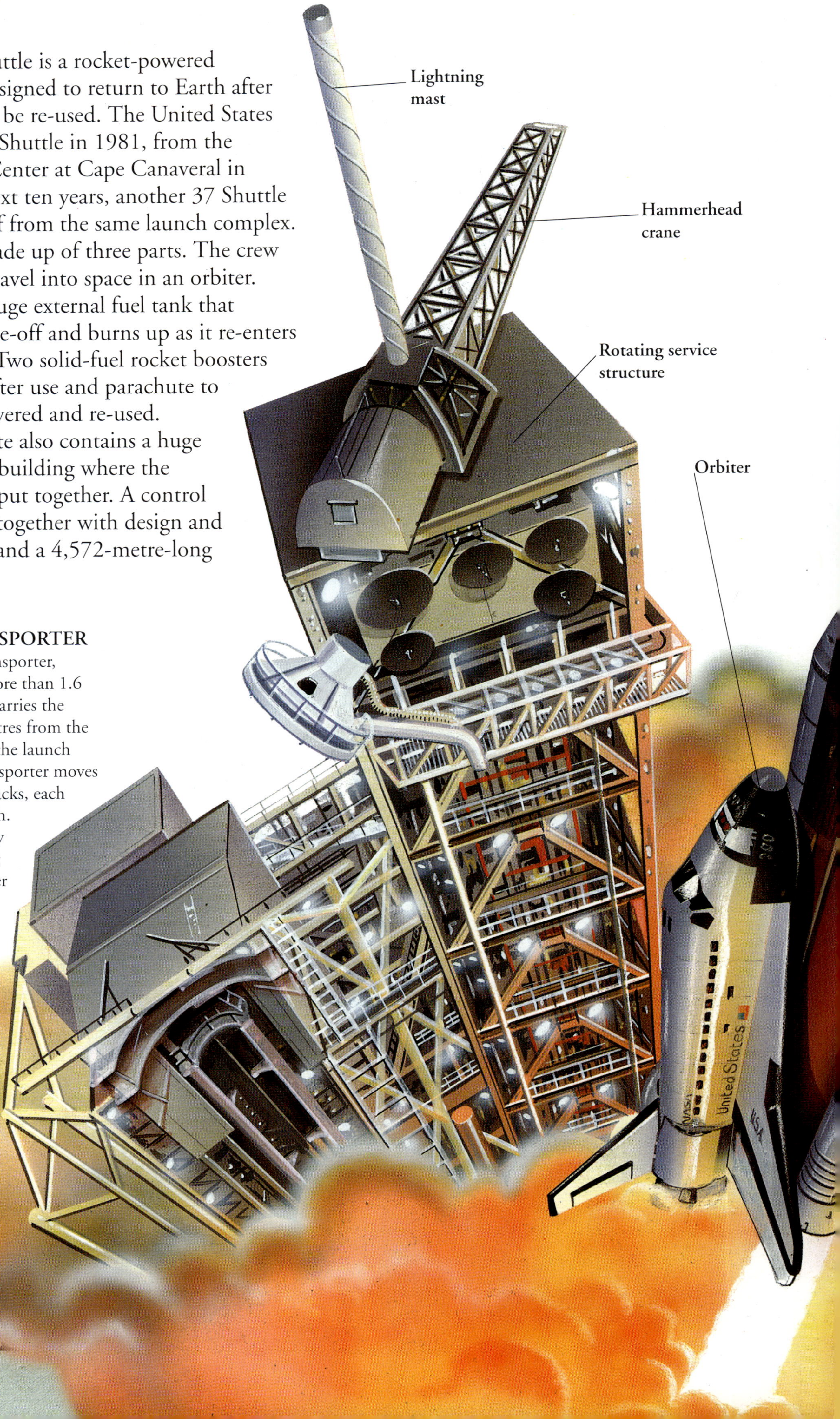

LAUNCH CONTROL

Scientists in the launch control room at Kennedy Space Center monitor the preparation and countdown to the launch. Once the Shuttle has risen above the launch tower, a few seconds after lift-off, control of the space flight passes to the Johnson Space Center in Houston, Texas.

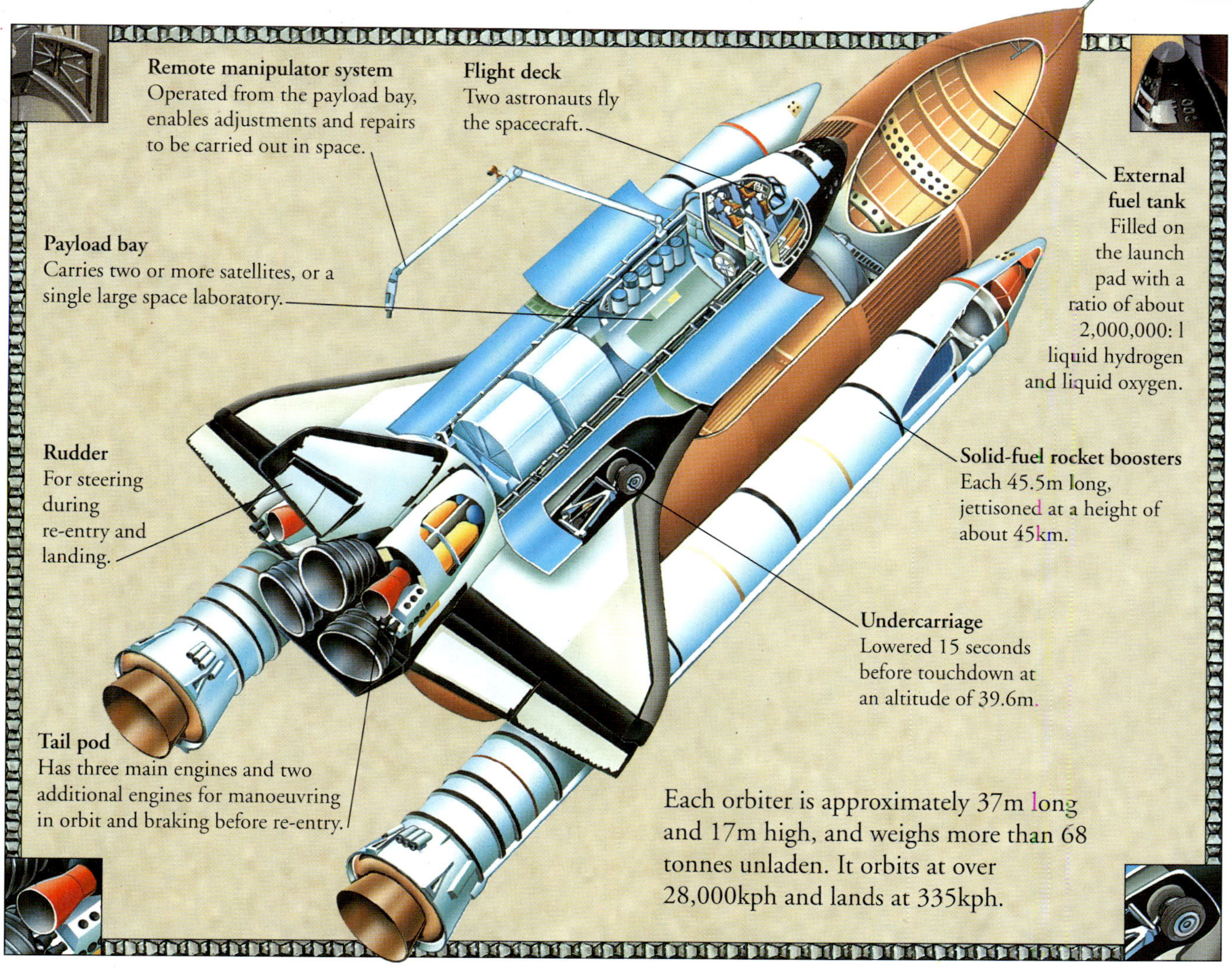

Each orbiter is approximately 37m long and 17m high, and weighs more than 68 tonnes unladen. It orbits at over 28,000kph and lands at 335kph.

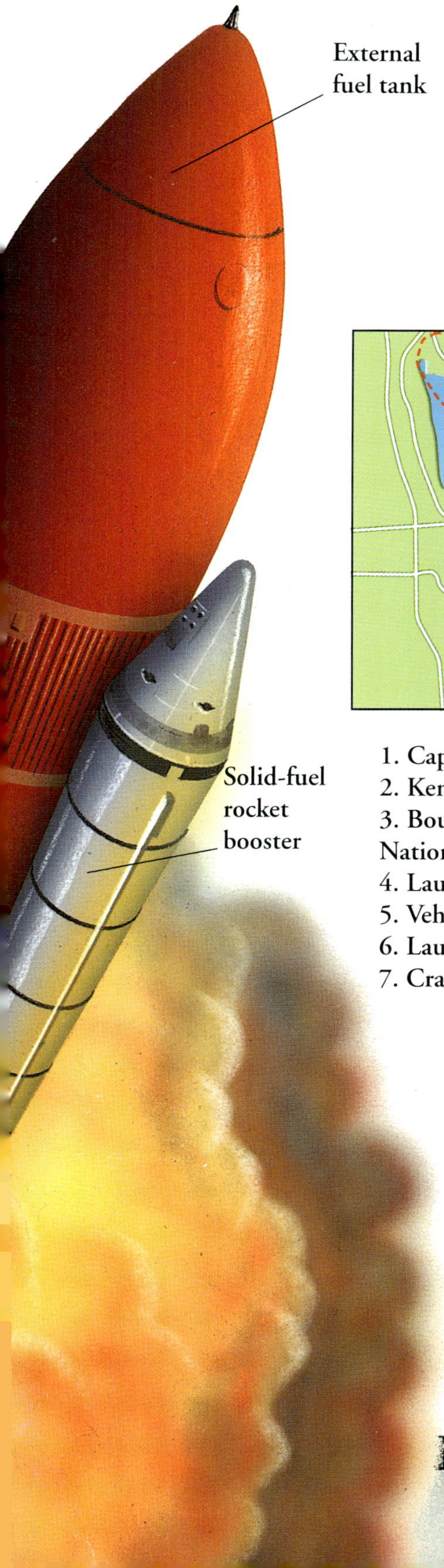

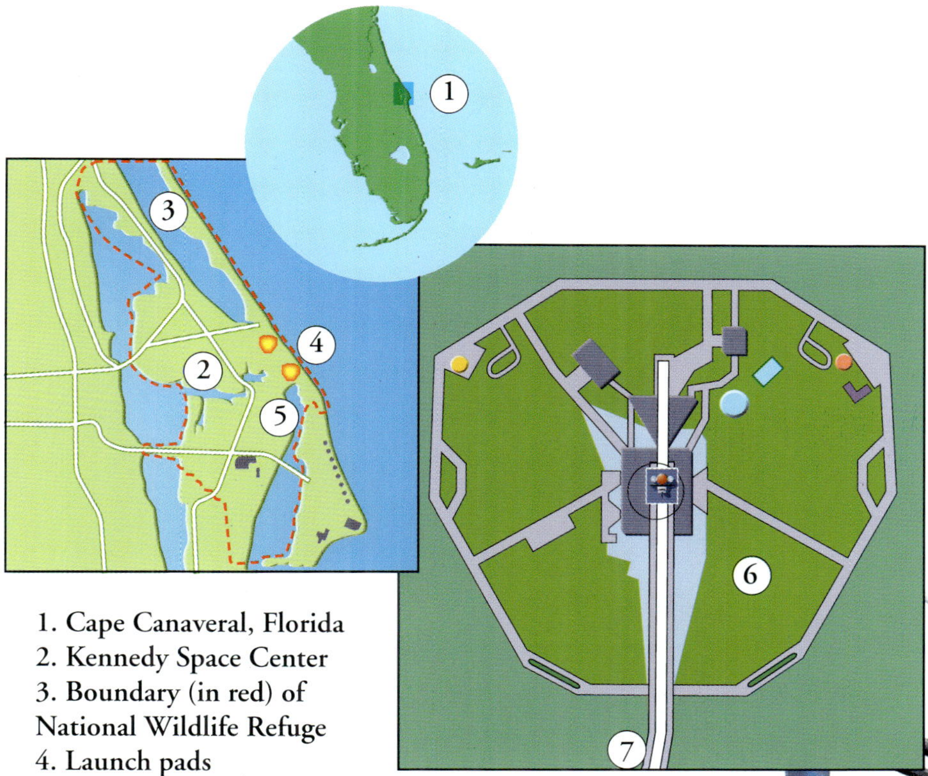

1. Cape Canaveral, Florida
2. Kennedy Space Center
3. Boundary (in red) of National Wildlife Refuge
4. Launch pads
5. Vehicle assembly building
6. Launch complex
7. Crawlerway

EMERGENCY!

If there is a fire when the Shuttle is on the launch pad, astronauts can escape from the orbiter by jumping into steel baskets attached to the service tower and sliding down cables to a concrete emergency shelter bunker 366 metres away. The descent takes approximately 35 seconds. A braking system using a net and drag chain stops the basket at the bottom.

VEHICLE ASSEMBLY

The vehicle assembly building at Kennedy Space Center is one of the largest buildings in the world. It is 160 metres tall, 218 metres long and 158 metres wide. Inside the building, the three separate units of the Shuttle vehicle – the external tank, the solid-fuel rocket boosters and the orbiter itself – are brought together before being transported to the launch pad. Sliding platforms inside the building allow workers to reach different levels during the assembly work.

Thames Barrier

"There was last night the greatest tide that ever was remembered in England to have been in this River, all Whitehall having been drowned."
Samuel Pepys' Diary, December 7th 1663

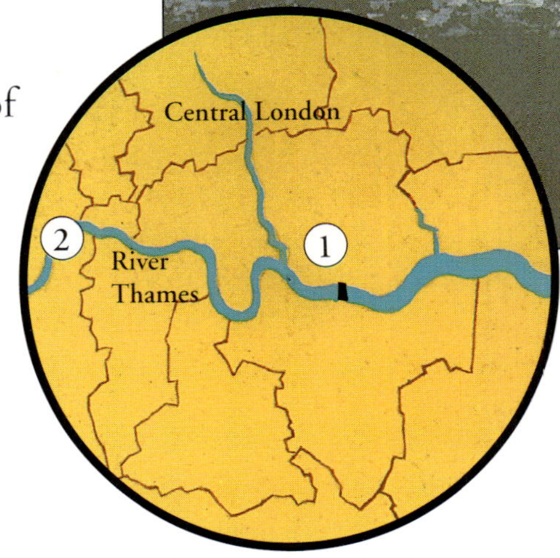

1. Thames Flood Barrier
2. Houses of Parliament

London, England's capital city, stands beside the River Thames. Areas of the city near the river have been close to disaster at least twice in the twentieth century. In 1928, fourteen Londoners were drowned in floods. Then in 1953, flood water along the river banks came only centimetres away from spilling over. The main threat of flooding comes from surges of water driven across the North Atlantic by cyclones. These surges usually pass north of Britain, but sometimes they sweep down the North Sea and into the Thames. Early in the 1970s, it was decided that London needed protection from possible floods. After 41 different schemes had been studied, the design of engineer Charles Draper was chosen.

In 1974, work started on a huge barrier across the Thames at Woolwich Reach, downstream from central London. The Barrier took eight years to complete. It consists of a series of steel gates that rest on the river bed when they are not needed, allowing ships to pass freely. When there is a flood alert, the gates are closed (raised) to form a 520-metre-wide wall of steel that holds back flood water.

RISING WATERS
The River Thames' high-water level has risen by about 75 centimetres each century. Experts who keep a careful watch on sea levels predict that they are likely to rise by about one metre each century in future.

LONDON'S NIGHTMARE
The great North Sea surge of 1953, which drowned over 300 people along the east coast of England, brought London to the edge of a disaster like the one imagined above. At the last moment, the cyclone that created the surge swept away towards continental Europe, and the water lapping the tops of the Thames embankments dropped.

CENTRAL GATES

This aerial view shows the four massive central gates. There are also four smaller gates to the north and two to the south. Each central gate is 61 metres wide, over 20 metres high, and weighs about 3,700 tonnes. Shell-like structures cover the machinery that closes (raises) and opens (lowers) the gates.

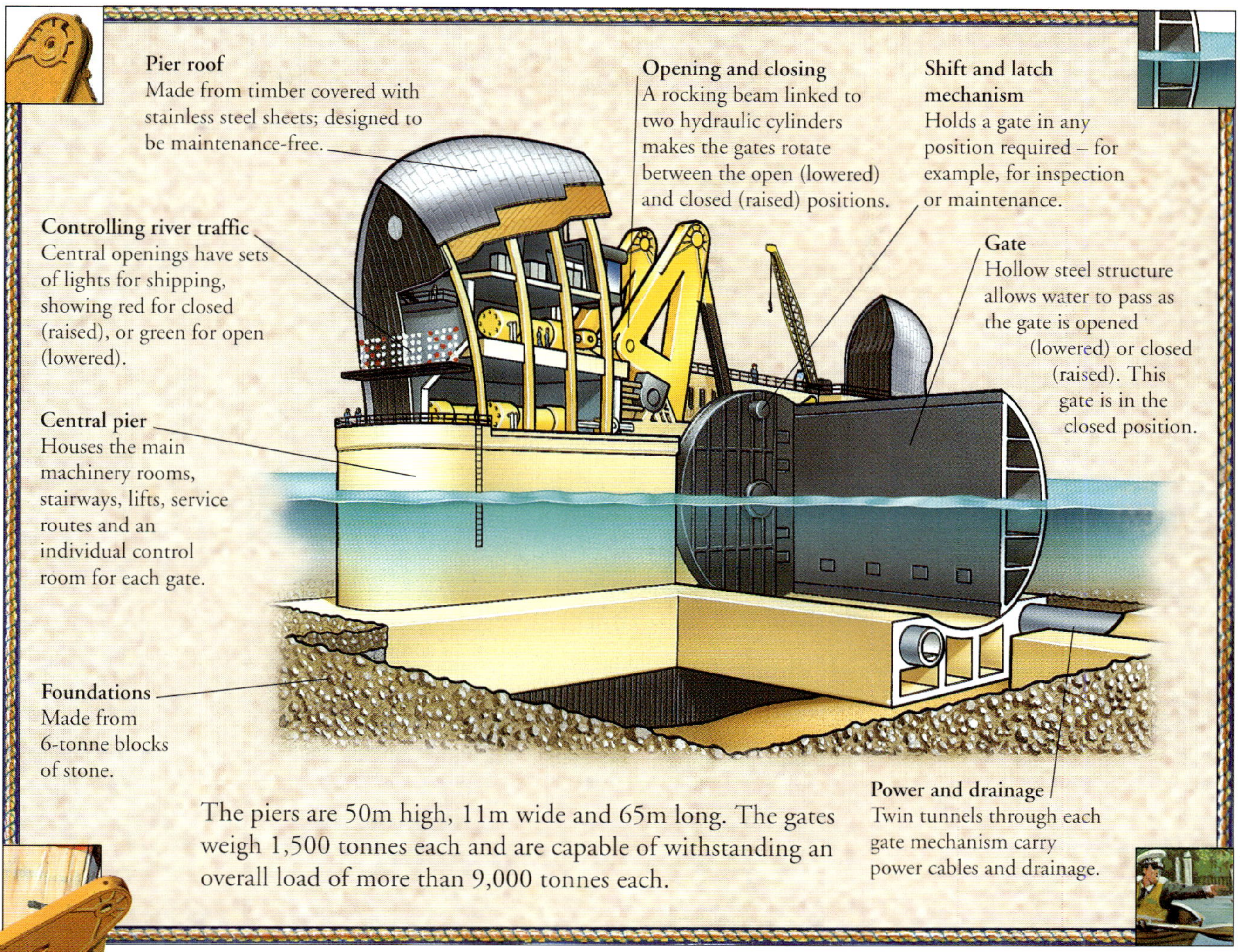

The piers are 50m high, 11m wide and 65m long. The gates weigh 1,500 tonnes each and are capable of withstanding an overall load of more than 9,000 tonnes each.

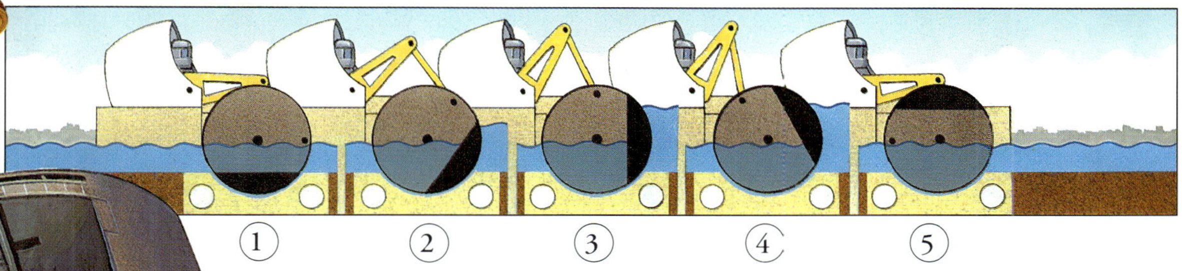

RAISING THE DEFENCES

When the Barrier is not in use, the gates rest in concrete sills on the river bed (1), allowing ships to pass between the piers. In a flood alert, the gates swing up (2) through 90 degrees (3), forming a barrier against the flood tide. They can also swing further, to allow some water underneath (4). For maintenance, the gates can swing right up (5). In the first 12 years of operation, the gates were raised over 20 times in response to flood warnings.

Channel Tunnel

"It is done, and we who were there at the doing of it can now look back and wonder that it got done."
Alastair Morton, co-chairman, Eurotunnel, 1994

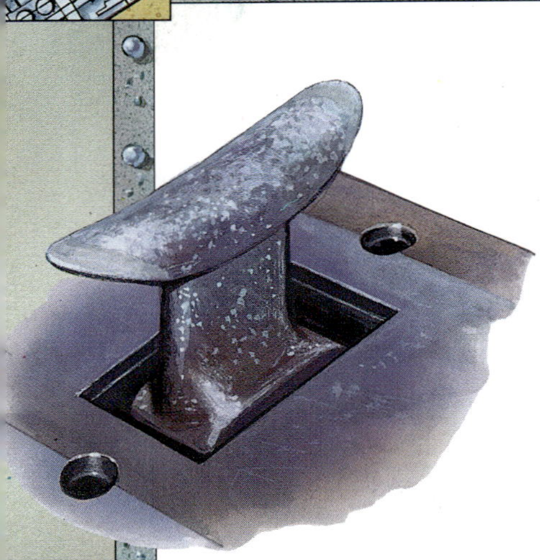

CUTTING PICK

The tunnel-boring machine (or TBM) can be fitted with different kinds of cutterhead. For dry rock picks are used. Each pick is made from hardened steel and cuts with a rocking action that provides the correct angle of attack for the cutting edge, while avoiding damage to the trailing edge.

The Channel Tunnel, linking England and France, carries passengers and vehicles by rail on a 50-kilometre journey that takes them under the English Channel. It was completed in 1993 after seven years of work, and was officially opened in 1994 by Queen Elizabeth II of the United Kingdom and President Mitterand of France. The Tunnel is Europe's largest single piece of engineering work. It is in fact three tunnels: two main tunnels and a smaller service tunnel between them. Both the French and the English trains use one of the main tunnels to travel in one direction, and use the other main tunnel to travel in the other direction. The service tunnel was built first. The French and British engineers, working from each end, met in the middle on December 1st 1990. Cars, coaches and lorries travel through the Tunnel on shuttle trains. They board and leave these at terminals that are linked to the major road systems of Britain and France. The train journey between the terminals takes just 35 minutes. Rail passengers can travel through the Tunnel on high-speed trains that link London, Paris and Brussels, as well as other cities on the route.

LINING THE TUNNEL

The lining of the main tunnels and the service tunnel is made from curved segments of reinforced concrete. These were manufactured on land and brought to the site ready for use. Each ring of segments is about 1.5 metres long. The rings were built starting with the lowest segment, and ending with the placing of a smaller key segment – holding the ring in position – in the roof. The joints were then sealed with special cement.

BREAKTHROUGH

Excitement grew among Tunnel workers during the autumn of 1990 as the French and British teams dug ever closer to each other. On December 1st, they made the breakthrough and demolished the last few centimetres of rock, creating the first land route between England and France for 12,000 years.

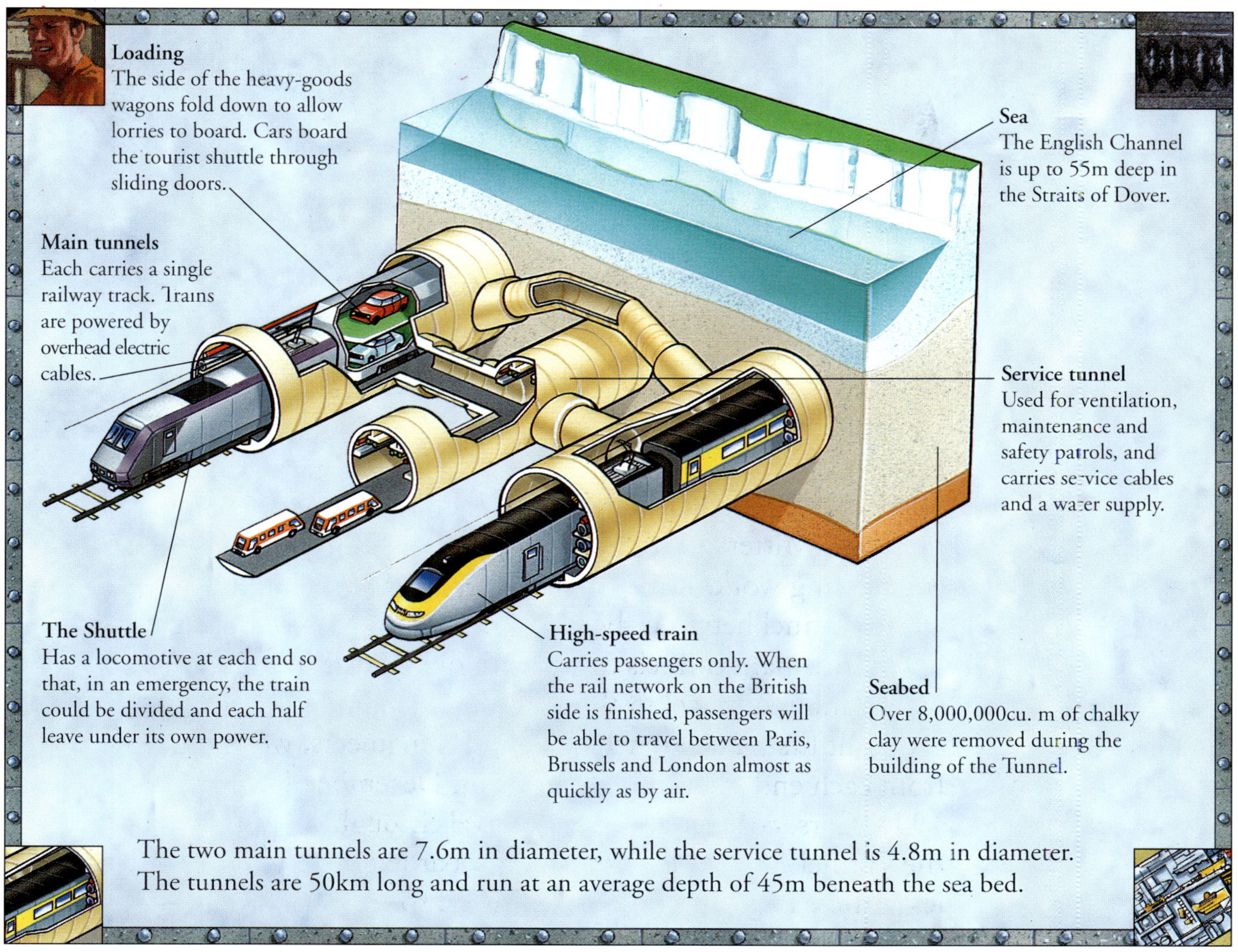

The two main tunnels are 7.6m in diameter, while the service tunnel is 4.8m in diameter. The tunnels are 50km long and run at an average depth of 45m beneath the sea bed.

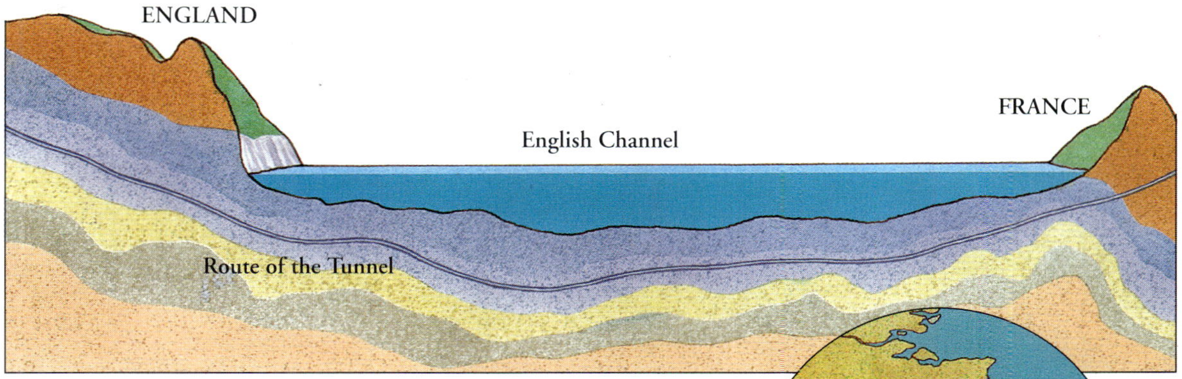

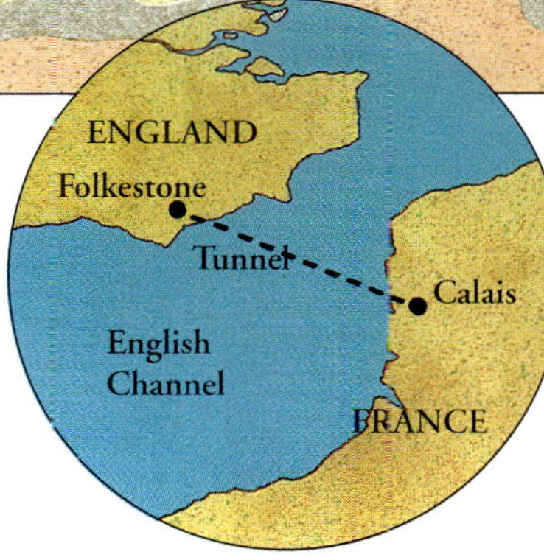

CROSS-CHANNEL ROUTE

The Tunnel connects Cheriton, near Folkestone on the English side, with Sangatte, near Calais in France. The section of the Tunnel under the sea bed is 38 kilometres long. The precise route was decided after engineers had studied data from over 100 boreholes.

THE TUNNEL-BORING MACHINE

Eleven giant tunnel-boring machines were used to dig the Tunnel through the chalky clay 50 metres below the sea bed. At the British end, the rock was mainly dry, and the cutterheads acted like a giant grater on the soft chalk. At the French end, water seepage from above made conditions more difficult. Mud often plastered the workers and clogged the equipment. The cutterhead was driven by giant hydraulic rams and steered by smaller side rams. Behind the cutterhead a conveyor belt carried the cut rock (called spoil) back to wagons for transporting to the surface. The Tunnel lining was put in place as the cutterhead moved along. Ventilation pipes carried air into the Tunnel and took out unwanted gases.

1. Cutterhead
2. Conveyor belt
3. Hydraulic power
4. Tunnel-lining equipment
5. Spoil-removal wagon
6. Ventilation pipes

Mir Space Station

PEACE SIGN

The *Mir* emblem shows the Space Station against a background of the Earth and stars, beneath the word *MIR*, which is Russian for "peace". The emblem is used on many items of equipment and on the crews' uniforms.

"As we came close, it looked like a white-winged seagull soaring above the world. Everything that contemporary technology can create is here."
Leonid Kizim, first commander of *Mir*, March 16th 1986

The *Mir* Space Station was launched in February 1986 by the then Soviet Union to study the long-term effects of living in space. It was designed so that its crew could live and work comfortably for long periods, and has even been described as a "space hotel". It has been occupied continuously by a succession of cosmonauts, some of whom have stayed for a year at a time. Since the launch of the base unit, new modules have been added, and linked in various positions, to enable various kinds of scientific experiments to be carried out. The *Kvant 1* module has specialised telescopes for studying space, while the *Kristall* module is a mini-factory used to produce flawless semiconductor crystals for use in electronics.

Two kinds of spacecraft travel between Earth and *Mir*. Unmanned *Progress* craft deliver supplies and take away rubbish. Crew members arrive and depart on *Soyuz* spacecraft. In 1995 there was a different visitor: history was made when a United States Space Shuttle docked at the Russian Space Station.

WALKING IN SPACE

Crew members of *Mir* sometimes need to go outside the Station to conduct experiments, inspect the modules or repair equipment. They put on spacesuits and a backpack. The backpack uses blasts of compressed air to help them move about. The cosmonauts remain tethered to the Station so that they cannot float off into space.

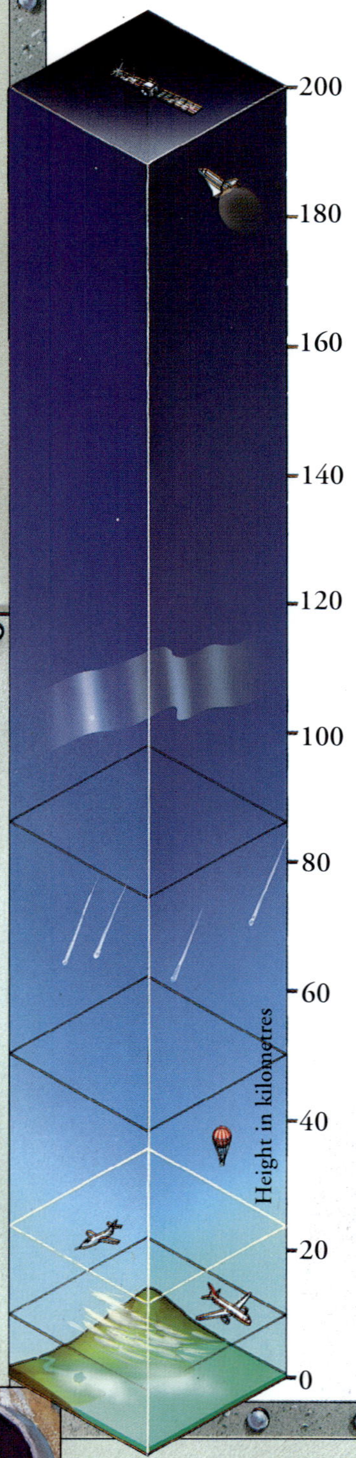

THE ATMOSPHERE

To travel into space, spacecraft have to overcome the pull of Earth's gravity. That is why huge rockets, blasting upwards at 40,000 kilometres per hour, are needed to launch a spacecraft. They must travel up through the Earth's atmosphere for over 200 kilometres before the spacecraft is free of gravity and can go into orbit.

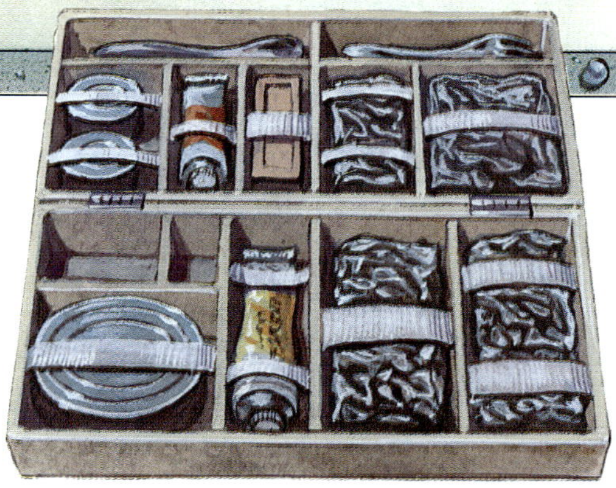

TIME TO EAT

Food for the *Mir* crew comes in tins or flexible packs similar to toothpaste tubes. Prepacked biscuits and bread are moistened to avoid crumbs, which would fly everywhere in the weightless conditions. Each food pack contains its own fork and spoon.

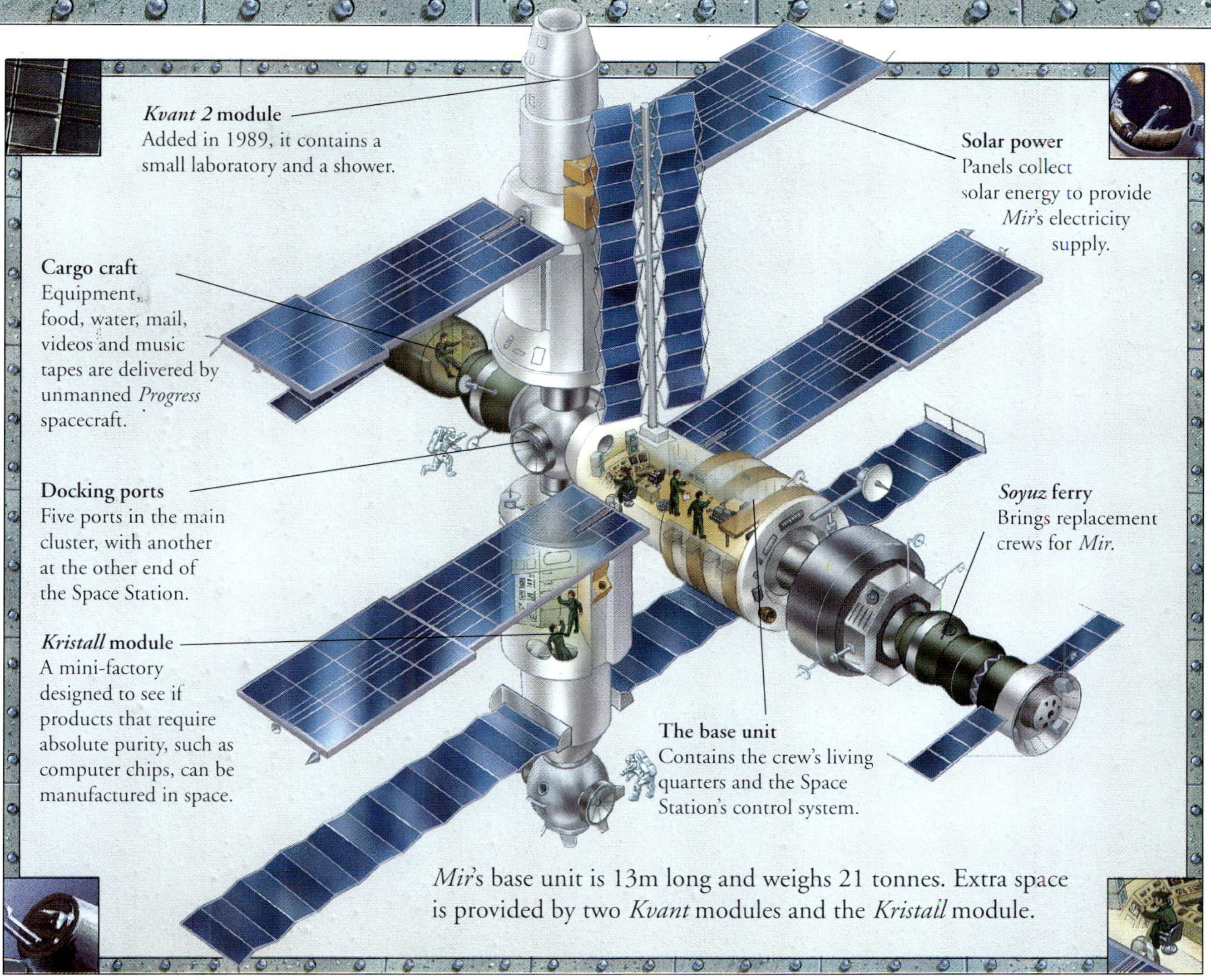

Mir's base unit is 13m long and weighs 21 tonnes. Extra space is provided by two *Kvant* modules and the *Kristall* module.

BEDTIME

Crew members are weightless while they are on board *Mir*, so they can sleep in any position. In the living quarters, visitors each have their own small cabin equipped with a sleeping bag attached to the wall. They zip themselves up to the neck, so that they don't float around while they are asleep. The crew member settling down for the night here is Helen Sharman, who in 1991 was chosen from hundreds of applicants to be the first British cosmonaut. She travelled to *Mir* in *Soyuz TM12*.

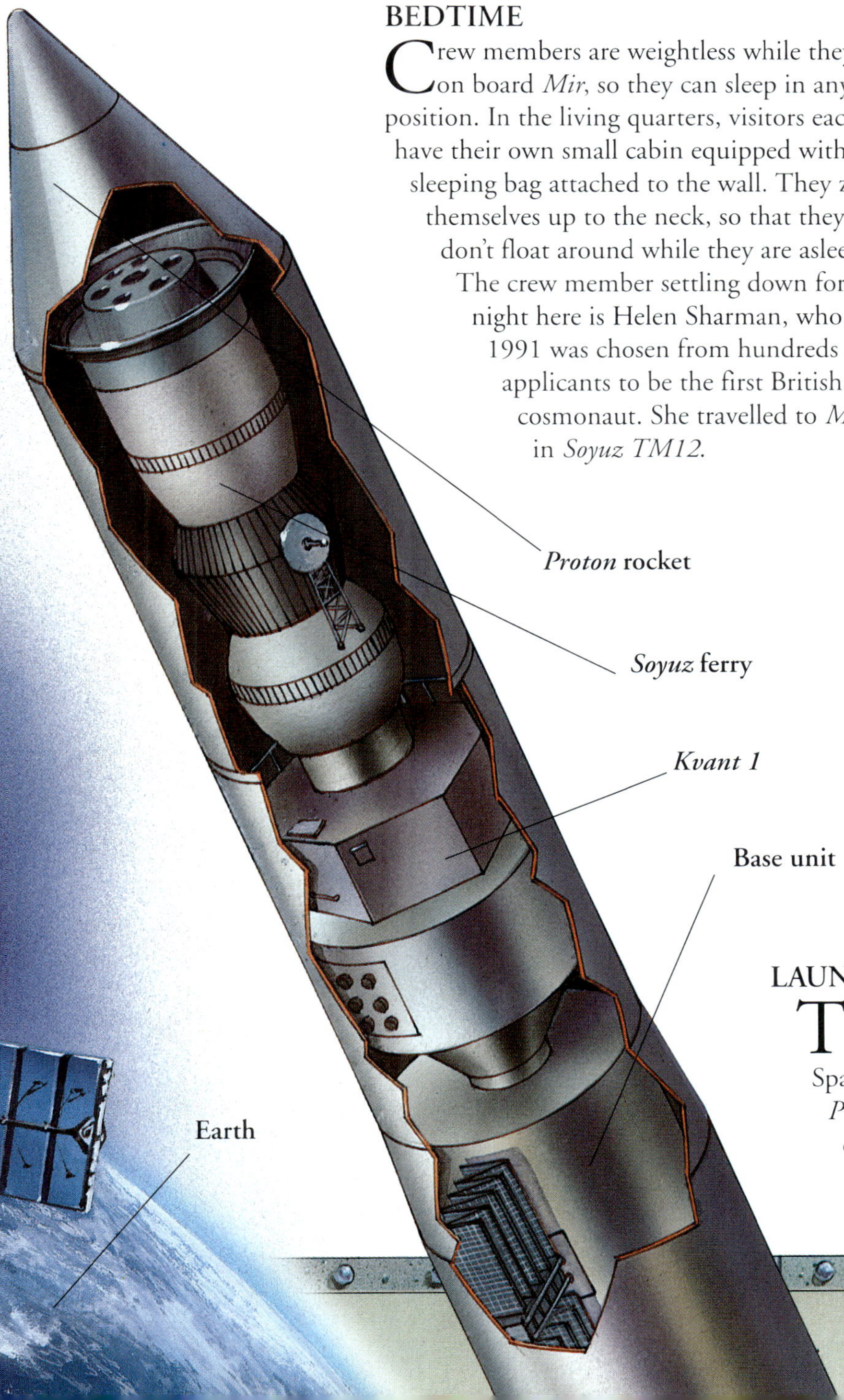

LAUNCHING MIR

The base unit of *Mir* was launched on February 20th 1986. The 21-tonne Space Station was lifted into orbit by a *Proton* rocket that was specially designed to carry heavy loads into space.The *Soyuz* ferry enabled the crew to return to Earth.

Gullfaks C

FLARE STACK

A build-up of excess gas from an oil rig's operations is a potential fire hazard. The excess gas is burned off on a flare stack sited well away from the production and living areas.

"Geologically speaking, the development and operation of the Gullfaks field is a great challenge. The company was confronted with the most complicated reservoir so far considered for production in the North Sea."
Statoil Information Department, 1990

Gullfaks is the name of a Norwegian oilfield in the North Sea between Britain and mainland Europe. Rising out of the sea above the oilfield is the Gullfaks C gas and oil production platform. Gullfaks C consists of a steel framework attached to four huge concrete pillars and a base, which rests on the sea bed 217 metres below the surface. It is 350 metres from the sea bed to the highest point of the rig. The framework is fitted with units called modules, which form the working and living quarters for a crew of 330. It also supports production equipment, derricks for loading and unloading goods, and a helicopter pad.

Natural gas was discovered under the North Sea in 1959, followed by oil in 1970, and since then numerous production platforms have been installed. Gullfaks C is the largest platform to date.

TAKING THE OIL ASHORE

Oil is transported away from Gullfaks C by tankers. They moor at special loading buoys close to the platform. Oil is stored in the rig's base and piped to the mooring buoys. Gullfaks C can produce 250,000 barrels of oil a day.

TALLER THAN THE EIFFEL TOWER

Standing 350 metres from the sea bed to its highest point, Gullfaks C is 50 metres taller than the famous Eiffel Tower in Paris, France.

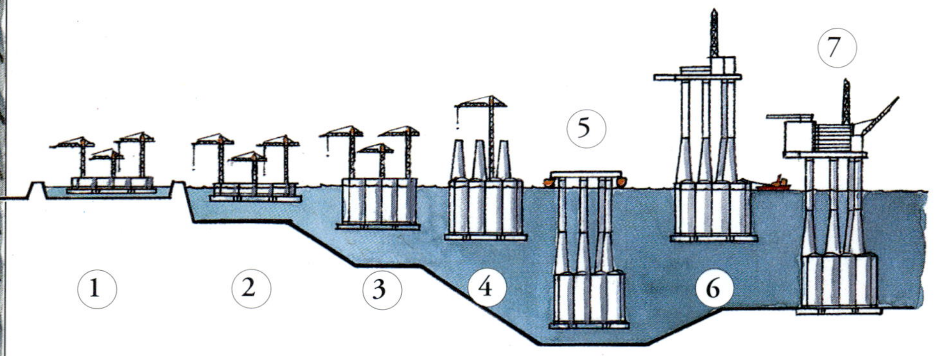

ASSEMBLING THE OIL RIG

There are seven key stages to erecting an oil rig. The hollow concrete supports, or caissons, which form the base of the rig are built in dry dock, towed out to sea and submerged. The rest of the rig is then added.

1. The caissons are built in dry dock.
2. The dock is flooded and the base is towed by tug into sheltered water.
3. As construction continues, the caissons are lowered by pumping in more water.
4. When the water level reaches the top of the caissons, concrete pillars are added.
5. The platform is built on top of the concrete pillars.
6. Water is then partly pumped out of the caissons, and the rig is towed by tug into its final position.
7. The caissons are filled with water and sunk to rest on the sea bed.

HELICOPTER LINKS

The crew of Gullfaks C travel to and from the Norwegian mainland, 175 kilometres away, by helicopter. The helicopter service also carries mail and small items of equipment. Food, technical supplies and heavier items of equipment are brought by a fleet of supply ships.

Gullfaks C is located 175km off the Norwegian coast. It extracts crude oil, which is refined into fuel for cars and aeroplanes. It is also a complete living environment for the crew, with its cabins and canteens.

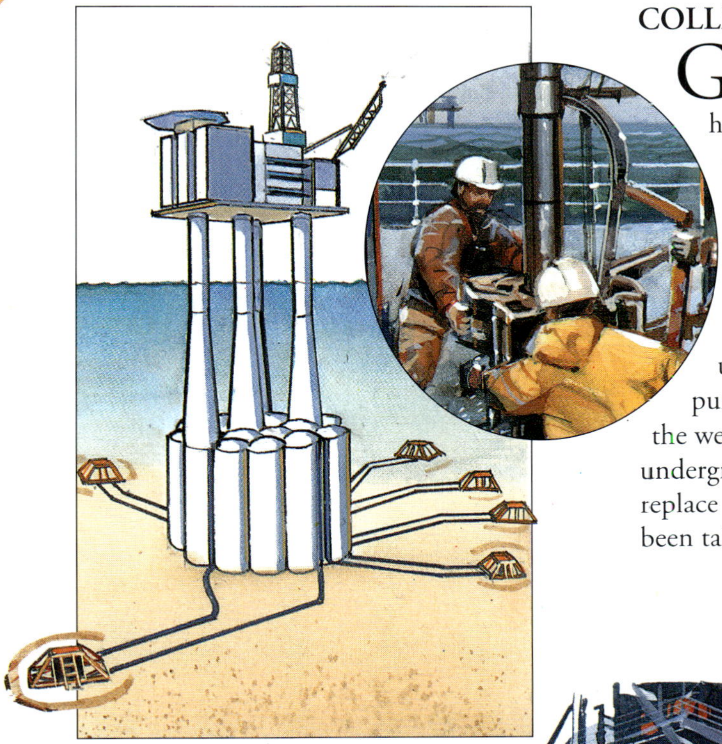

COLLECTING OIL

Gullfaks C extracts oil from wells that have already been drilled on the sea bed. Pipelines from the platform connect to the wellheads. They pump the oil upwards and also pump water through the wellheads into the underground reservoirs to replace the oil that has been taken out.

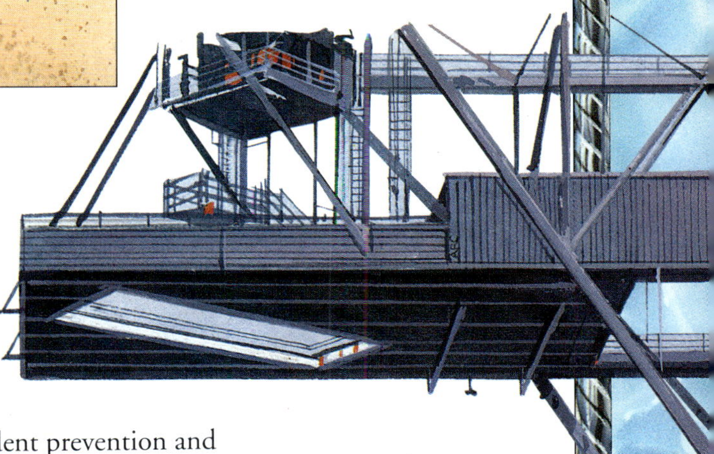

SAFETY MEASURES

Safety is a major priority on oil rigs. Crews are trained in evacuation procedures, fire fighting, accident prevention and first aid, and there are regular emergency drills. Gullfaks C is equipped with "free-fall" lifeboats that drop from the rig to the sea 30 metres below, thus saving valuable time in an emergency. On reaching the water, the lifeboats automatically stabilise themselves and quickly cruise to safety.

White-knuckle ride

"This is the most significant structure in Blackpool since the Tower was built a century ago. It is the best steel rollercoaster in the world."
Geoffrey Thompson, Managing Director, Blackpool Pleasure Beach, 1994

Nearly 72 metres high, the Pepsi Max Big One at Blackpool Pleasure Beach, England, is the world's tallest and fastest rollercoaster. Its three trains carry visitors for a stomach-churning two-minute ride of over 1,600 metres at speeds of up to 136 kilometres per hour. Opened in 1994, the Big One is a wonder of structural engineering. Engineers had to calculate precisely the forces exerted on the track and the steel framework supporting it as the trains hurtle round the Big One's tight vertical and horizontal bends. Because of these forces, passengers feel up to four times heavier than their true weight at a number of points during the ride.

At full capacity, trains leave the station at intervals of 63 seconds. This amazing ride can be enjoyed by a total of 1,700 people every hour.

LIGHTING UP

In addition to the floodlights that illuminate the Big One after dark, aircraft warning beacons are mounted on the structure. These are needed because of the ride's height and the fact that Blackpool's airport is not far away.

PUTTING ON THE BRAKES

There are four braking units like the one shown below, one at the station and three on the track itself. One half of the brake unit remains in a fixed position, and the other half moves. As each car passes over the brake unit, the moving part clamps on to a fin attached to the base of the car between the wheels. The brakes are used to trim the train's speed or to stop the train.

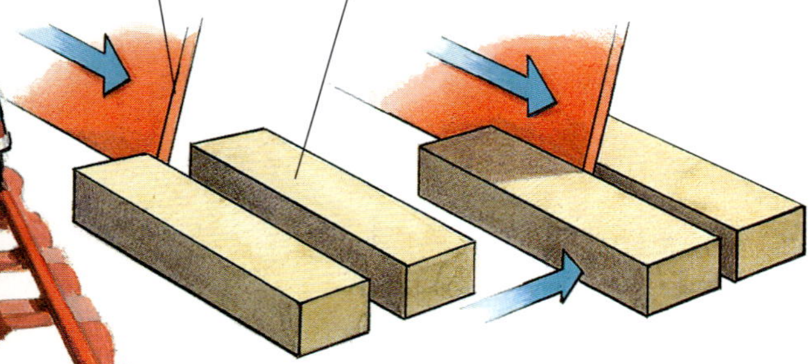

VITAL STATISTICS

The ride is supported by 94 monopods and 237 stanchions. To overcome the effects of corrosion from salt and sand in the sea air, protective paint is regularly applied.

Ride takes about two minutes

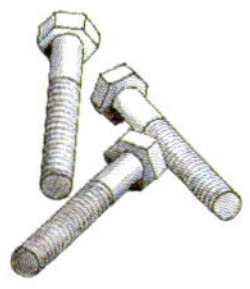

Over 60,000 bolts used in construction

2,600 tonnes of steel were used (equal to 64km if laid end to end)

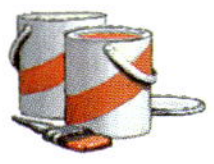

35,000sq. m of surface area were painted with five coats of paint

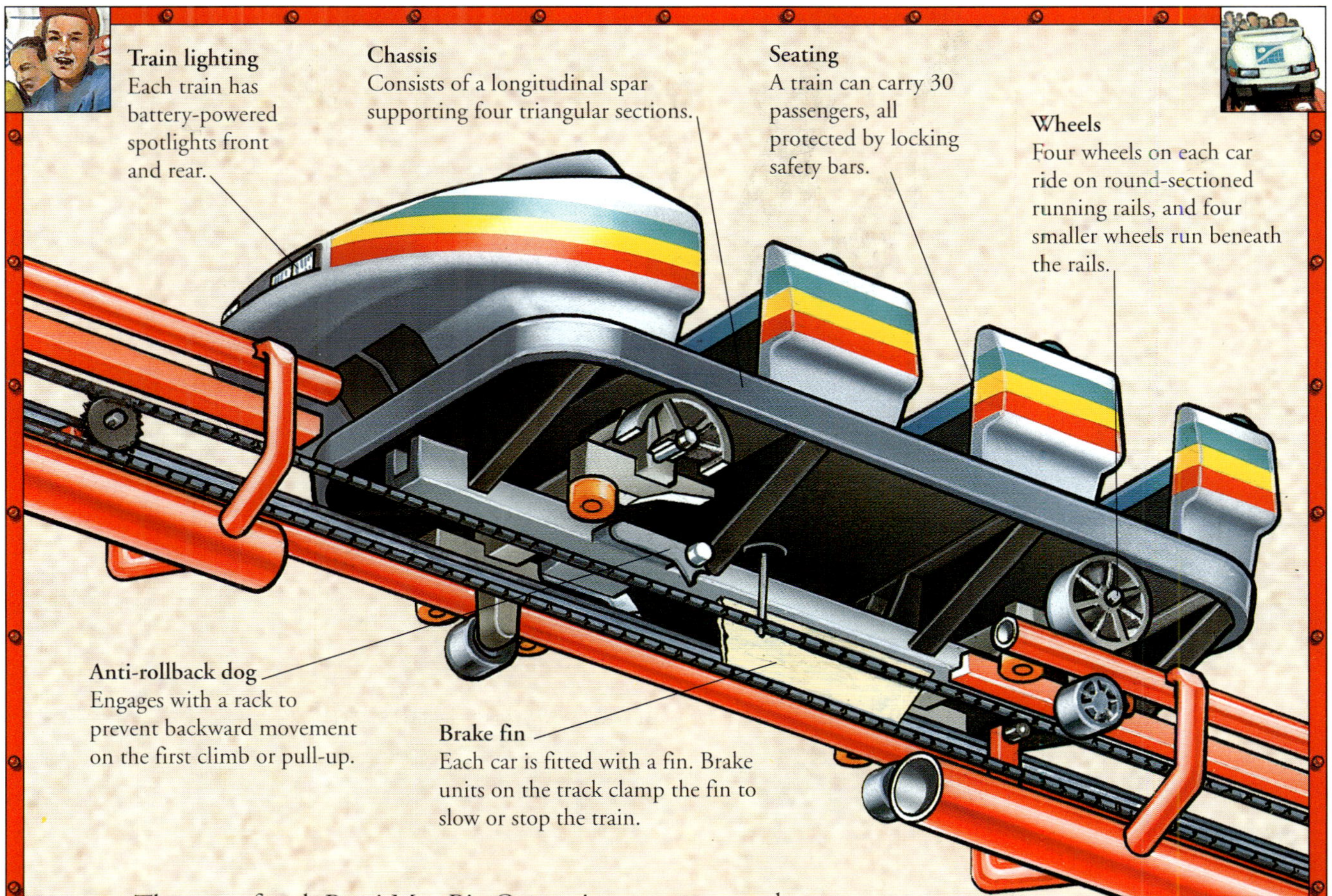

The cars of each Pepsi Max Big One train are permanently coupled, giving an overall length of 15.9m and an unloaded weight of 5,623kg.

ALL THE FUN OF THE FAIR

The 72-metre-high Big One towers above all the other rollercoaster rides – both wooden and steel – in the park.

USING GRAVITY

At the top of a slope, a stationary rollercoaster train (1) has energy. This energy, called potential gravitational energy, can be used to move downhill at speed. Once the train starts moving down the slope (2), this turns into the kinetic energy of motion, which carries the train to the top of the next slope (3). There it changes back to potential energy. The top of each slope has to be slightly lower than the one before it because the train loses some of its energy to friction against the track and to air resistance.

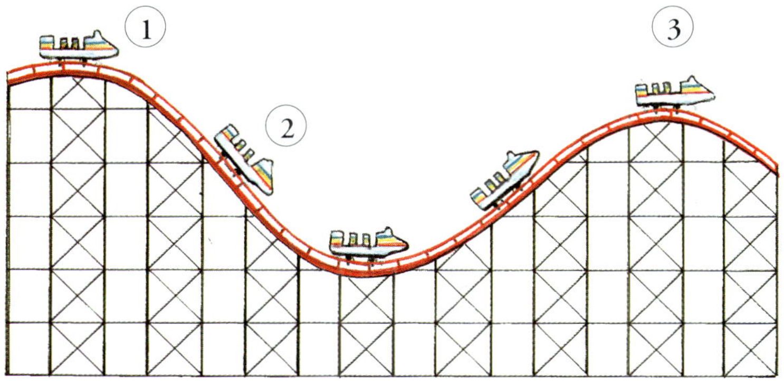

UPHILL CLIMB

At the starting station, the train attaches to a moving chain that pulls it up the first steep incline. Two devices called chain dogs on the second and fourth cars engage with the chain, and as the chain moves the train is pulled up the incline. At the crest of the first drop, a release mechanism on the track detaches the chain dogs from the chain, and the train hurtles downhill at an angle of 65 degrees.

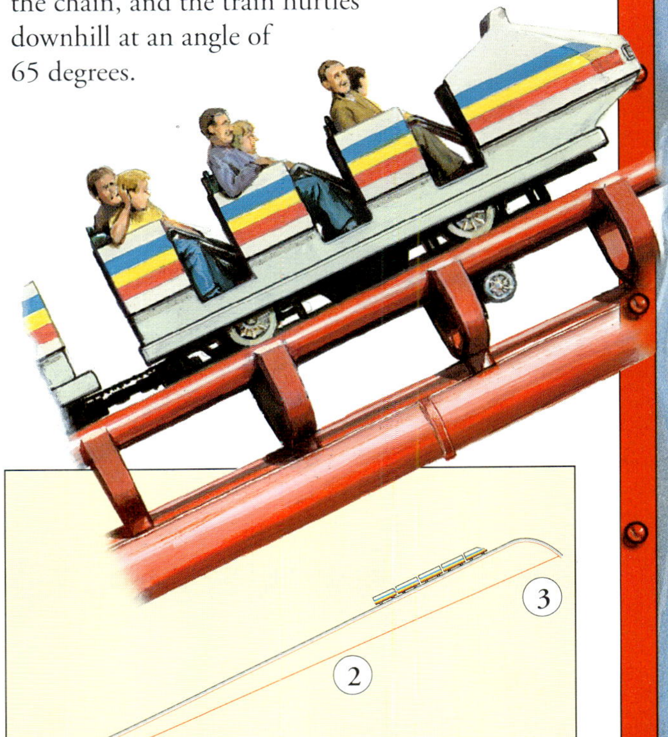

1. Motor to drive the chain
2. Moving chain attached to the track
3. Chain-release point

GLOSSARY

amphitheatre
An open structure built for large numbers of spectators to watch gladiatorial contests and other entertainments. Amphitheatres were built in many of the cities of the Roman Empire.

amplify
To make louder and stronger.

antenna
Metal rod or wire used to receive or transmit electronic signals.

aqueduct
A bridge-like structure designed to carry water overhead.

Art Deco
A modern, highly coloured, streamlined style of decoration that was developed during the 1920s and was widely used on buildings, furniture, furnishing materials and domestic goods such as plates and cups.

awning
A temporary roof made of canvas or other cloth that can be placed in position and removed as required.

azimuth
An imaginary line drawn from the point in the sky immediately above an observer's head to the horizon.

beacon
A fire lit at a highly visible point, usually to pass on a warning about enemy troop movements. Chains of beacons, lit in turn, could carry messages over long distances.

borehole
A hole drilled in the ground by engineers to obtain a core of the underlying rock, which can then be studied to find out what lies beneath the ground surface.

box
An open-sided enclosure in a theatre or an amphitheatre for use by important spectators.

buoy
A float anchored at sea to mark an underwater hazard or for use as a mooring.

buttressed
Any structure supported by pillars of brick or stone. A flying buttress is a special kind of supporting arch or partial arch that is most commonly seen in cathedrals.

caisson
A watertight case of metal or concrete, often used as a foundation for underwater structures.

cantilever
A beam, firmly anchored and weighted down at one end, that is able to support another beam at its free end.

capstone
The topmost stone of a structure (such as a pyramid), often ornately decorated.

cast iron
A type of iron that is run into moulds when it is molten and then allowed to set.

cathedral
A Christian church, usually very large, which contains the throne of a bishop.

chain dog
A revolving cog wheel attached to a vehicle; it engages with a chain and provides the driving force for the vehicle.

china clay
A fine white powder extracted from the ground for use in making pottery.

chisel
A hand-tool with a stone or metal end, used to shape stone or wood.

compressed-air drilling machine
A drill (sometimes called a pneumatic drill) driven by compressed air which, as it expands, provides the power to drill holes in rock.

concrete
A mixture of sand, gravel and cement used in building.

conveyor belt
A continuously moving endless belt that carries waste material from an excavation to waiting trucks for transport to a disposal site.

corrosion
Damage caused to metal structures by the chemical action of the atmosphere or sea water. Rust, the reddish-brown deposit which affects iron, is an example of corrosion.

counterweight
An extra weight that is fitted to a heavy object to balance the object's weight and to help control its movement.

cross-braced
Fitted with diagonal spars of metal to give added strength to a structure.

crude oil
Thick, syrupy oil that is pumped from an oil well. Crude oil is then "cracked" or processed to remove impurities and separate different thicknesses of oil for various uses.

cutterhead
A mechanically driven revolving tool at the front of a drilling machine that can be fitted with a variety of cutting picks, drills and teeth to perform different cutting and drilling tasks.

cyclone
A system of winds that revolves round a low pressure area. The winds can reach very high speeds and sometimes cause damage to structures and trees, even large ones.

Declaration of Independence
An agreement signed on July 4th 1776 by the founders of the United States of America. It announced that the country was no longer a British possession, and stated the rules by which the United States would be governed.

derrick
A fixed crane used to raise and lower drill tubes over an oil well.

dolerite
A hard rock, sometimes containing fragments of a glass-like substance, used in the Iron Age to make cutting tools.

dynamite
A safe explosive based on nitroglycerine and invented by the Swedish chemist Alfred Nobel in 1866. It is detonated using a lit fuse or by a charge of high-voltage electricity.

embankment
An artificial riverbank built of earth or stone to prevent water from flooding nearby land.

emplacement
A small structure that contains a cannon or other large mechanical weapon and gives protection to the gun crew that mans it.

encoder
A device that changes electronic signals into a form in which they can be transmitted or interpreted.

generator
A machine for producing electricity by rotating a coil of wire in a magnetic field. The energy to drive the generator is provided by steam pressure from an oil, coal, gas or nuclear fuel furnace, or by wind, wave or solar power.

girder
A beam of iron or steel used as a support in structures, usually formed into a T or L shape to give added strength.

gold leaf
A decorative material made by beating gold (a soft metal) into very thin sheets.

granite
A hard volcanic rock that resists the effects of weathering and corrosion.

gravity
A force on the Earth that acts on objects close to the Earth and pulls them towards its centre. Rockets used in space launches have to be powerful enough to enable spacecraft to overcome the force of gravity and reach space, where gravity is no longer effective.

gunpowder
A mixture of chemicals and charcoal invented by the Ancient Chinese. It was the only known explosive until the 19th century.

hand-tool
A tool used to cut and shape wood and stone. It is operated without the use of machinery.

hanger
A steel cable suspended from the arch of a bridge to support the bridge's deck.

hard hat
A protective helmet worn by building workers to shield them from objects falling on their heads. It is now required by law in many countries.

headroom
The space underneath the deck of a bridge or the roof of a tunnel that enables ships or automobile traffic to pass through.

herald
An official in a Roman amphitheatre who made announcements at the start of the programme and helped keep the spectators in order.

hurricane
A storm with winds that exceed 120kph.

hydraulic
Operated by the pressure of a liquid such as oil or water.

inscription
Words cut into the stone of a monument, often recording when and by whom it was built.

limestone
A stone that has been used for building from the earliest times because it can be cut and shaped using only simple tools.

lock
A device that enables vessels using waterways to change levels. The vessel moves into a position on the waterway and watertight gates are shut in front of and behind it. The water level between the gates is then raised or lowered to match the level in the next lock or stretch of water. The gates in front of the vessel are opened and it moves forward at the new level.

mallet
A hammer, usually with a wooden head, used to tap or cut stone or bricks into position.

marble
A hard, durable form of limestone that can be carved and polished.

module
A section of a building or structure that is made in a factory and then transported to the site where it is to be used.

mooring
A place where a ship or airship can be anchored or tethered. Airships can not take off or land like winged aircraft. They moor at tall masts, and passengers and crew embark or disembark while the airship is tethered to the mast by ropes.

mortar
A mixture of lime, sand and water used to join stones or bricks together. It is applied wet, and when it dries makes a hard bond between adjoining surfaces.

mummy
A dead body (usually human but sometimes animal) soaked in oils and other chemicals and then bound tightly in cloth to preserve it. The Ancient Egyptians mummified their kings in the belief that this would ensure life after death.

murmillo gladiator
One of the classes of gladiators who fought before audiences in the Roman Empire. Murmillo gladiators were heavily armed with helmets, swords and shields.

navigable
A body of water, natural or artificial, that is sufficiently wide and deep to be used by ships.

optical telescope
A telescope that gathers light from a distant object and presents an image to the observer through a system of lenses and mirrors.

parabolic
Bowl-shaped.

parapet
A wall built along the top of fortifications to give protection to soldiers.

payload
Cargo.

pedestal
The base supporting a column, pillar or statue.

persecution
The deliberate, systematic ill treatment of people by their government or society.

pre-stressed concrete
Concrete poured over wires which are then tightened before the concrete hardens. The set concrete holds the stressed wires in place and this gives added strength. Pre-stressed concrete was invented by a French engineer, Eugene Freyssinet, in 1930.

pulley
A grooved wheel used with a rope to lift heavy loads with minimum effort. Pulleys may be fixed in a block attached to a structure, or moveable as in a crane or derrick.

reinforced concrete
Concrete strengthened by being poured over a network of metal wire. It was invented by a French gardener, Joseph Monier, in 1868 as a way of strengthening garden ponds and flower pots.

reservoir
A large natural or artificial store for liquids.

restoration
Work carried out on a structure to return it to its original condition.

retiarius gladiator
One of the classes of Roman gladiators. Retiarius gladiators wore only a short tunic or apron and carried a three-pronged spear and a net. Their aim was to trap their opponents in the net and then kill them with the spear.

rivet
A device for fastening two pieces of metal together. A rivet consists of a length of steel which is passed through holes in the pieces of metal. The ends of the pieces are then beaten flat to make the fastening.

rollercoaster
A high-speed fairground ride that carries passengers in open carriages along a very steeply inclined and tightly curved track.

semiconductor
A solid substance that conducts electricity at high temperatures but acts as an insulator at low temperatures. Semiconductors are used in many electronic devices such as radios, televisions and videos.

skyscraper
A tall modern building. There is no definition of how tall a building must be to be called a skyscraper, but the Home Insurance Building in Chicago, built in 1885 and only ten storeys high, is regarded as the world's first.

spoil
The general term for waste material from building and engineering works.

square
An L-shaped tool used by builders and carpenters to check right angles.

subreflector
Part of a radio telescope that collects radio signals bounced off the parabolic reflector and focuses them before passing them on to the radio receiver.

surge
A sea condition created when strong winds blowing onshore prevent the high tide from receding, so that the next high tide adds to the previous one.

terracotta
Baked clay.

tunnelling shield
A tool used to protect workers building a tunnel. It consists of a steel cylinder with rotating cutting tools at its closed front end and metal sections behind, forming the closure.

vaulted
Supported by a series of arches radiating from a central point.

ventilation
Any method of supplying fresh air and extracting stale air and poisonous gases.

weightless
The condition of a person or object that is temporarily not affected by gravity. Spacecraft and their crews are weightless once they have escaped from the Earth's gravitational pull.

wellhead
A fixture attached to the seabed at the top of a borehole and connected by pipeline to an oil production platform. Pumps at the wellhead carry crude oil to the platform and return water to the well to replace the oil taken out.

winch
A method of raising or lowering heavy loads by turning a wheel which carries a rope.

wrought-iron
Iron that is compressed by being passed through rollers while it is still semi-molten (very hot and semi-liquid). This process increases its toughness and resistance to corrosion.

INDEX